So lernst du mit Lighthouse

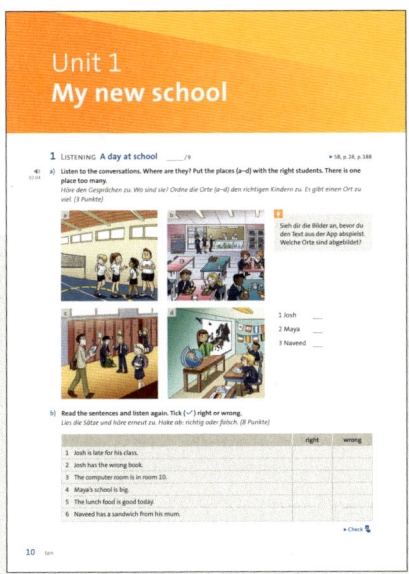
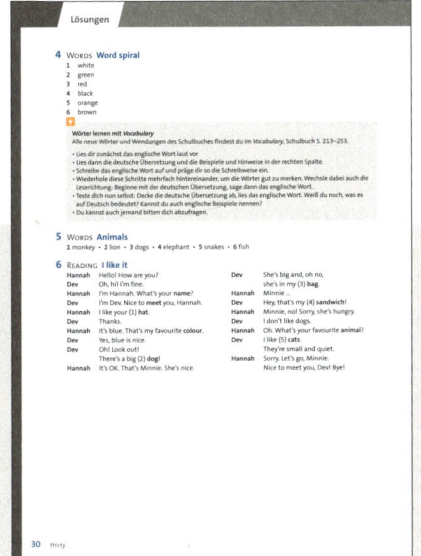
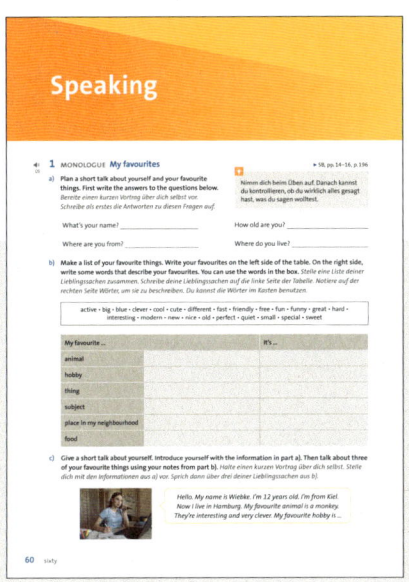

Dein Klassenarbeitstrainer hat fünf Units

In jeder Unit findest du Aufgaben zu verschiedenen Kompetenzen, die dich auf deine Klassenarbeit vorbereiten. Mit Hilfe der Tabelle am Ende jeder Unit kannst du deine Ergebnisse überblicken.

Überprüfe deine Lösungen

In der Mitte des Heftes findest du die Lösungen zu den Aufgaben. Hier findest du auch Lerntipps, um dich optimal auf deine Klassenarbeit vorzubereiten. Diese Seiten kannst du heraustrennen.

Sprechen üben

Vielleicht wirst du eine mündliche Klassenarbeit haben. Zwischen Units 4 und 5 findest du die *Speaking*-Unit. Hier kannst du Monologe und Dialoge üben. Danach kannst du dir die Lösungsbeispiele anhören und deine Ergebnisse überprüfen.

Diese Symbole und Hinweise geben dir Orientierung.

___/15	▶ SB p. 21, p. 183	▶ More help, p. 73
Neben den Aufgaben findest du die maximale Punktzahl, dort kannst du deine erreichten Punkte eintragen.	Dieser Verweis zeigt dir, dass sich das Thema auf die Seiten 21 und 183 in deinem Schulbuch bezieht.	Dieser Verweis führt dich zum *More Help*-Kapitel, wo du zusätzliche Hilfen für die *Writing*-Aufgabe findest.

Lerntipps zur Vorbereitung auf eine Klassenarbeit findest du auf Seite 78–79.

Deinen Klassenarbeitstrainer findest du auch in der Cornelsen Lernen App

Siehst du eines dieser Symbole in deinem Klassenarbeitstrainer, kannst du in deiner App …

  Erklärfilm

▶ Check

alle Hörtexte und Erklärfilme aufrufen.

deine Antworten überprüfen, falls du die Lösungsseiten nicht zur Hand hast.

BASIC lighthouse 1

Klassenarbeitstrainer

Im Auftrag des Verlages erarbeitet von
Marc Proulx, Berlin; Ulrike Rath, Aachen

In Zusammenarbeit mit der Englischredaktion
Klaus Unger (Projektleitung), Chelsea Ledvinka-Heß, sowie
Elizabeth Pancake-Steeg, Chiara Castellano, Julian Theo Wacker

Beratende Mitwirkung
Katharina Pick, Wülfrath

Lizenzmanagement
Silke Kirchhoff

Illustrationen
Evelt Yanait, Advocate Art
Irina Zinner, Hamburg

Fotos
Anja Poehlmann, Brighton

Umschlaggestaltung
Rosendahl, Berlin

Layoutkonzept
Klein & Halm, Berlin

Layout und technische Umsetzung
Straive

Audio-Dateien
Studio
Clarity Studio, Berlin
Regie und Aufnahmeleitung
Susanne Kreutzer
Tontechnik
Gislinde Böhringer, Susanne Kreutzer, Dimitris Kritikos

Druck
Athesiadruck GmbH

PEFC-zertifiziert
Dieses Produkt stammt aus nachhaltig bewirtschafteten Wäldern und kontrollierten Quellen
PEFC/18-31-166 www.pefc.de

www.cornelsen.de

Soweit in diesem Lehrwerk Personen fotografisch abgebildet sind und ihnen von der Redaktion fiktive Namen, Berufe, Dialoge und Ähnliches zugeordnet oder diese Personen in bestimmte Kontexte gesetzt werden, dienen diese Zuordnungen und Darstellungen ausschließlich der Veranschaulichung und dem besseren Verständnis des Buchinhaltes.

Dieses Werk berücksichtigt die Regeln der reformierten Rechtschreibung und Zeichensetzung.

Die Webseiten Dritter, deren Internetadressen in diesem Lehrwerk angegeben sind, wurden vor Drucklegung sorgfältig geprüft. Der Verlag übernimmt keine Gewähr für die Aktualität und den Inhalt dieser Seiten oder solcher, die mit ihnen verlinkt sind.

Alle Drucke dieser Auflage sind inhaltlich unverändert und können im Unterricht nebeneinander verwendet werden.

© 2023 Cornelsen Verlag GmbH, Berlin

Das Werk und seine Teile sind urheberrechtlich geschützt. Jede Nutzung in anderen als den gesetzlich zugelassenen Fällen bedarf der vorherigen schriftlichen Einwilligung des Verlages.

Hinweis zu §§ 60 a, 60 b UrhG: Weder das Werk noch seine Teile dürfen ohne eine solche Einwilligung an Schulen oder in Unterrichts- und Lehrmedien (§ 60 b Abs. 3 UrhG) vervielfältigt, insbesondere kopiert oder eingescannt, verbreitet oder in ein Netzwerk eingestellt oder sonst öffentlich zugänglich gemacht oder wiedergegeben werden. Dies gilt auch für Intranets von Schulen.

1. Auflage, 1. Druck 2023
978-3-06-034594-6

lighthouse 1
BASIC
Klassenarbeitstrainer

Deinen Klassenarbeitstrainer findest du auch in der **Cornelsen Lernen App**.
Siehst du eines dieser Symbole in deinem Klassenarbeitstrainer, findest du in der App …

- alle **Audios**
- alle **Erklärfilme**
- **Lösungen** zu den Aufgaben

Cornelsen

Vorwort

Vorwort für Eltern

Sie möchten Ihrem Kind ein sicheres Gefühl für die Klassenarbeiten geben?
Der Klassenarbeitstrainer hilft Ihrem Kind beim Lernen.

Dear Parents,

in den Klassenarbeiten Ihrer Kinder werden die Fertigkeiten Hörverstehen (*Listening*), Leseverstehen (*Reading*), Wortschatz (*Words*), Grammatik (*Language*), Mediation, Lernen lernen (*Study skills*) und Schreiben (*Writing*) abgefragt. Mit dem Klassenarbeitstrainer kann Ihr Kind diese Fertigkeiten gezielt trainieren. Für jede Unit finden Sie verschiedene Aufgaben zu den einzelnen Fertigkeiten.

Im Klassenarbeitstrainer finden Sie darüber hinaus ein Kapitel mit Übungen zur Fertigkeit Sprechen (*Speaking*).

Vorbereitung
Vergewissern Sie sich, dass Ihr Kind sich mindestens eine Woche vor der Klassenarbeit genau über die relevanten Themen informiert. Mit einem Lernplan kann Ihr Kind festlegen, wann welche Fertigkeit geübt wird. Eine Vorlage dafür finden Sie auf Seite 79.

More help-Aufgaben
Schreiben stellt für Schülerinnen und Schüler eine besondere Herausforderung dar. Das Kapitel *More help* stellt zusätzliche Hilfen (*useful phrases, switchboxes, etc.*) für die *Writing*-Aufgaben zur Verfügung.

Speaking-Aufgaben
Zwischen den Units 4 und 5 finden Sie Übungen zur Fertigkeit Sprechen (*Speaking*). Manche dieser Übungen kann Ihr Kind allein bearbeiten, andere am besten mit einem Partner (z. B. Klassenkameraden). Damit Sie die Ergebnisse mit den Lösungsvorschlägen vergleichen können, sollte sich Ihr Kind beim Sprechen aufnehmen. Beispielhafte Antworten werden in diesem Klassenarbeitstrainer auch als Audioformat zur Verfügung gestellt.

Lösungen
Wenn eine Aufgabe bearbeitet wurde, kann diese mit den Lösungen aus dem herausnehmbaren Lösungsheft verglichen werden. Achten Sie beim Vergleichen genau darauf, welche Fehler gemacht wurden, und überlegen Sie mit Ihrem Kind, wie diese beim nächsten Mal vermieden werden können. Neben den Beispiellösungen enthält das Lösungsheft auch Lerntipps und die Skripte zu den Hörtexten. Die Bewertungstabelle am Ende jeder Unit hilft Ihnen dabei, den Lernstand Ihres Kindes besser einschätzen zu können.

Achtung
Natürlich enthält jede Unit mehr Aufgaben als eine normale Englischarbeit. Es ist also normal, dass Ihr Kind für die Bearbeitung einer Unit im Klassenarbeitstrainer länger braucht als für eine normale Arbeit.

Wir wünschen viel Spaß beim Lernen und eine erfolgreiche Klassenarbeit.
All the best

Inhalt

So lernst du mit Lighthouse	1
Impressum	2
Vorwort für Eltern	4
Inhaltsverzeichnis	5
Hello! Nice to meet you	6
Unit 1 My new school	10
Unit 2 My family and home	16
Unit 3 My day	22
Lösungen	29
Unit 4 Where I live	53
Speaking	60
Unit 5 Enjoy!	66
More help	73
So bereitest du dich auf eine Arbeit vor	78
Quellenverzeichnis	80
Übersicht Audio-Tracks	U3

Hello!
Nice to meet you

1 LISTENING Four Kids ____ / 12 ▶ SB, p. 15, p. 184

🔊 01 **a) Listen and match the sentence parts.**
Höre zu und verbinde die Satzteile. (3 Punkte)

1 Magda is
2 Amir is
3 Ben is
4 Tanya is

A twelve years old.
B from Plymouth.
C eleven and from Ireland.
D from London.
E ten years old.
F from Germany. He's twelve years old.

(Magda is — A twelve years old; Magda is — D from London)

b) Listen again. Circle their favourite colours. Are the hobbies right (✓) or wrong (✗)?
Höre noch einmal zu. Umkreise die Lieblingsfarben der Kinder. Sind die Hobbys richtig (✓) oder falsch (✗)? (9 Punkte)

💡 Sieh dir die Bilder genau an, bevor du den Text aus der App abspielst. Dann weißt du, worauf du beim Hören achten musst und die Lösung fällt dir leichter. Du kannst dir die Texte auch noch einmal hören.

1 Magda
dancing ✗
music ✓
blue / (red) / green

2 Amir
reading ☐
dancing ☐
orange / red / pink

3 Ben
TV ☐
swimming ☐
yellow / green / blue

4 Tanya
music ☐
TV ☐
white / green / blue

▶ Check

6 six

Hello!

2 WORDS What about you? ____ / 10   ▶ SB, p. 16

Look at the pictures and the words in the box. Complete the sentences.
Schaue auf die Bilder und den Wortkasten. Vervollständige die Sätze und beantworte die Fragen.

> animal • hobby • colour • sport • thing

1 My favourite _____ is _____.

2 My favourite _____ is a _____.

3 My favourite _____ is my _____.

4 My favourite _____ is _____.

5 My favourite _____ is _____.

3 WORDS Word pairs ____ / 4   ▶ SB, pp. 202–206

Look at the first word. Put the letters of the second word in the correct order to make opposites.
Sieh dir das erste Wort an. Bringe die Buchstaben des zweiten Wortes in die richtige Reihenfolge um das Gegenteil zu bilden.

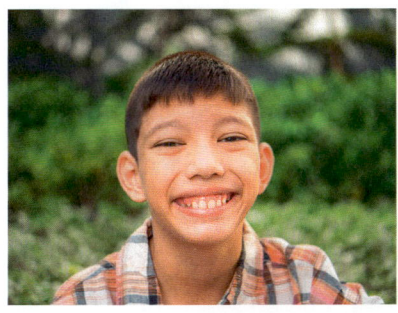

1 bad – **dogo**   *good*

2 close – **pnoe** _____

3 big – **lmasl**   _____

4 right – **ogrnw** _____

5 old – **wne**   _____

▶ Check

Hello!

4 WORDS Word spiral   ___ / 6   ▶ SB, p. 184

Find six colours in the spiral and write them down.
Finde sechs Farben in der Spirale und schreibe sie auf.

1 _____
2 _____
3 _____
4 _____
5 _____
6 _____

5 WORDS Animals   ___ / 6   ▶ SB, p. 14, p. 185

Look at the animals. What are they? Complete the words.
Schaue dir die Bilder an. Welche Tiere sind abgebildet? Vervollständige die Wörter.

It's a m __ __ __ __ __.

It's a l __ __ __.

They are d __ __ __.

It's an e __ __ __ __ __ __ __.

They are s __ __ __ __ __.

It's a f __ __ __.

▶ Check

Hello!

6 READING I like it ____ / 9   ▶ SB, pp. 15–16

Complete the dialogue with the numbered pictures and the words in the box.
Vervollständige die Dialoge mit den nummerierten Bildern und mit den Wörtern im Kasten.

> animal • colour • meet • name

Hannah	Hello! How are you?
Dev	Oh, hi! I'm fine.
Hannah	I'm Hannah. What's your _____?
Dev	I'm Dev. Nice to _____ you, Hannah.
Hannah	I like your (1) _____.
Dev	Thanks.
Hannah	It's blue. That's my favourite _____.
Dev	Yes, blue is nice.
Dev	Oh! Look out! There's a big (2) _____!
Hannah	It's OK. That's Minnie. She's nice.
Dev	She's big and, oh no, she's in my (3) _____.
Hannah	Minnie …
Dev	Hey, that's my (4) _____!
Hannah	Minnie, no! Sorry, she's hungry.
Dev	I don't like dogs.
Hannah	Oh. What's your favourite _____?
Dev	I like (5) _____. They're small and quiet.
Hannah	Sorry. Let's go, Minnie. Nice to meet you, Dev! Bye!

▶ Check

Unit 1
My new school

1 LISTENING A day at school ___/9   ▶ SB, p. 28, p. 188

🔊 02-04

a) **Listen to the conversations. Where are they? Put the places (a–d) with the right students. There is one place too many.**
Höre den Gesprächen zu. Wo sind sie? Ordne die Orte (a–d) den richtigen Kindern zu. Es gibt einen Ort zu viel. (3 Punkte)

> 💡 Sieh dir die Bilder an, bevor du den Text aus der App abspielst. Welche Orte sind abgebildet?

1 Josh ___

2 Maya ___

3 Naveed ___

b) **Read the sentences and listen again. Tick (✓) right or wrong.**
Lies die Sätze und höre erneut zu. Hake ab: richtig oder falsch. (8 Punkte)

		right	wrong
1	Josh is late for his class.		
2	Josh has the wrong book.		
3	The computer room is in room 10.		
4	Maya's school is big.		
5	The lunch food is good today.		
6	Naveed has a sandwich from his mum.		

▶ Check

2 WORDS What can you see? ____/9   ▶ SB, p. 21, p. 175

Kayla's bag is open. What can you see? Complete the answers.
Kaylas Tasche ist offen. Was kannst du sehen? Vervollständige die Antworten.

1	a	*pencil case*
2	a	r_____
3	a	g_____
4	a	p_____ s_____
5	an	ex_____ b_____
6	a	p_____
7	an	o_____
8	a	r_____
9	an	a_____
10	an	En_____ b_____

3 WORDS History lesson ____/8   ▶ SB, pp. 207–208

It's a history lesson with Ms Lopez. Complete the sentences with the words in the box.
Es ist Geschichtsunterricht bei Frau Lopez. Vervollständige die Sätze mit den Wörtern im Kasten.

> answer • be • book • can • don't • go • help • open

Ms Lopez	Good morning, students. Quiet, please.
Beth	_____ I open the window, please?
Ms Lopez	Yes, you can. Now find your history _____ and …
Maya	Sorry I'm late, Ms Lopez.
Ms Lopez	OK, Maya, but don't _____ late again. Now listen, class. _____ your book at page …
Emilia	Ms Lopez, can I _____ to the toilet, please?
Ms Lopez	Yes, you can.
Maya	What page is it, Sophie?
Sophie	I don't know.
Ms Lopez	_____ talk! Let's start now. It's page 12. Read the text. Then _____ the questions.
Sophie	This is hard. Can you _____ me?
Ms Lopez	Yes, I can.

▶ Check

4 LANGUAGE **My timetable** ____/11 ▶ SB, pp. 176–177

Santi writes an email to her friend Esme in London. Put in: *I, you, he, she, it, we,* or *they*.
Santi schreibt eine E–Mail an ihre Freundin Esme in London. Füge ein: I, you, he, she, it, we, *oder* they.

to: esme@example.net
from: santi@example.net

Hi Esme,

My timetable this year isn't bad. _____ 'm lucky. Design is my favourite subject. _____ 's very cool. _____ have music and art too. My teachers aren't bad. _____ 're friendly. Mr Williams is my music teacher. _____ can sing and play the guitar. _____ think that's really cool. Suriya is in my class too. Do _____ remember Suriya? _____ 's great. After music, Suriya and I go to the canteen. _____ always see Jonas and Dev there. We like them. _____ 're nice. Yeah, my school is OK. How are _____ ? How is your timetable?

Bye, Santi

5 LANGUAGE **Three students** ____/16 ▶ SB, pp. 24–25, p 177

Complete the texts. Use the words in the boxes.
Vervollständige die Texte. Benutze die Wörter in den Kästen.

1 | are • isn't • 're • is • 'm |

Hi, I _____ David. My school _____ great. It _____ big. I like that. Computing and PE _____ my favourite classes. They _____ on Thursday.

2 | 's • 'm • 'm not • 're • aren't • is |

Hi, I _____ Kezia. I _____ from Brighton. Brighton _____ new for me. It _____ nice here. The kids at school _____ mean. They _____ really friendly.

3 | 're • are • isn't • 'm • 's |

Hello, I _____ Annie. Charlie and Ahmad _____ my school friends. We _____ in the same history class. History _____ my favourite subject, but it _____ fun with Charlie and Ahmad.

▶ Check

6 Reading At Winford School ____/6 ▶ SB, p. 27, p. 197

Read about the students at Winford School. Who says what? Tick (✓) the right person.
Lies, was die Schülerinnen und Schüler der Winford School sagen. Wer sagt was? Setze einen Haken in den passenden Kästchen.

---

www.winfordschool.example.edu

Meet some Winford School students

Home   Students   Teachers   Subjects   Activities   Calendar   Links

Hi, I'm Kezia. I'm from Manchester. It's nice here in Brighton. I like the sea and my new school is great.
My favourite day is Tuesday. On Tuesday morning lesson one is English. Then I have music and then art. I eat lunch with my new friend, Nick. After lunch we have PE in the sports hall.

Hi, my name is Nick. I'm in class 7A.
My favourite lessons are geography and history. They're on Monday. Geography is lesson four and history is lesson five after lunch. I like Friday too. It's cool because lesson one is music.

Hello, I'm Annie. I'm from Edinburgh. I'm in class 7C. Our teacher is Mr Obayo. He's our science teacher too.
Wednesday is my favourite day of the week. I have science, then in lesson four I have design and technology. After lunch I have my favourite subject – French.

Hi, I'm David. My mum and dad are from London, but I'm from Brighton. I'm in class 7E. I like our school. It isn't very big and that's good.
I don't have a favourite day of the week, but Monday isn't bad. In the morning, lesson one is computing. After lunch I have PE.

	Kezia	Nick	Annie	David
1 I have music on Friday morning.				
2 After lunch on Monday I go to the sports hall.				
3 I have French after lunch on Wednesday.				
4 I like Tuesdays because I have music and art.				
5 My class teacher is my science teacher too.				
6 My two favourite lessons are on Monday.				

▶ Check

1

7 LANGUAGE What's wrong? ___/8 ▶ SB, p. 177

Correct the sentences. Use short forms.
Korrigiere die Sätze. Benutze die Kurzformen.

1 Davi's favourite sport is swimming.

   It *isn't* swimming. It's _____ football.

2 Cora is ten years old.

   She _____ ten. She _____ nine.

3 Charlie: Am I late?

   Erin: No, you _____ late. You _____ on time.

4 Mira and Raina are in the computer room.

   They _____ in the computer room. They _____ in the canteen.

5 You're from Brighton, right?

   No, I _____ from Brighton. I _____ from _____.

8 WORDS School topics ___/8 ▶ SB, p. 34

Find and circle the words for the things in the pictures.
Finde die abgebildeten Wörter und kreise sie ein.

subjects

people

S	T	U	D	E	N	T	P	C
T	O	L	C	K	D	V	H	L
V	E	L	O	D	S	S	E	A
G	N	A	G	M	A	T	H	S
P	E	N	C	I	L	S	I	S
F	C	O	V	H	W	J	O	R
A	F	B	G	I	E	M	L	O
U	Q	E	R	R	N	R	G	O
B	I	N	P	U	A	G	L	M
M	K	W	L	L	Z	P	L	M
C	A	N	T	E	E	N	H	O
O	S	C	H	R	V	F	E	Y

school things

places

▶ Check

14 fourteen

9 WRITING An email to a friend   ____/15

▶ SB, p. 26–27

Write an email to your English friend Jamie. Tell him about your school.

▶ More help, p. 73

Schreibe deinem englischen Freund Jamie eine E-Mail. Erzähle ihm von deiner Schule.

You can write about:
- your timetable
- your favourite subjects
- what you like at school
- your teachers
- your friends at school
- ...

---

to   Jamie@example.net

subject   My school

Hi Jamie,

Today I want to write to you about my school. The name of my school is _____

I'm in class _____. My favourite teacher is _____

He/ She _____. The kids at my school are/aren't _____.

My timetable is very_____. My favourite lesson is _____.

My friends at school are _____.

Thats my school!

Bye,

_____

Bereich	Aufgabe	erreichte Punktzahl		🤩	😎	🤔	😭
listening	1	____/9		9–8	7–6	5	4–0
reading	6	____/6		6	5	4–3	2–0
words	2	____/9					
	3	____/8	____/25	25–23	22–18	17–13	12–0
	8	____/8					
language	4	____/11					
	5	____/16	____/35	35–32	31–25	24–18	17–0
	7	____/8					
writing	9	____/15		15–14	13–11	10–8	7–0
Gesamt		____/90		90–81	80–63	62–45	44–0

▶ Check

Unit 2
My family and home

1 Reading My family ____ / 6

▶ SB, p. 44, p. 189

Arlo is Emily's new classmate. It's lunch break and they're in the canteen.
Arlo ist Emilys neuer Klassenkamerad. Es ist Mittagspause und sie sind in der Kantine.

Arlo … so that's my family. What about yours?
Emily My mum's name is Erica. She's a teacher, but not at our school. My dad's name is Rory. He has a clothes shop. He's from Ireland. Mum and Dad live in different places.
Arlo Oh, that's sad.
Emily No, it's fine. They have new partners. I live with my dad and his partner, Steve. I really like Steve. He's very funny.
Arlo That's cool. Is your mum's partner nice?
Emily Yes, he is. That's Enrico. At the weekend I go to their place. They have a nice, modern flat in Bristol. And there's Grandma Lynn and Grandpa Mike. They live near me. They're my mum's parents. They have two dogs, three rabbits and a beardie.
Arlo Wow. What's a beardie?
Emily It's a lizard. Her name is Lulu. She's my favourite. The pets live in their house and in the garden. Their garden is so messy!
Arlo Hm. What about your dad's parents?
Emily Grandpa Liam lives in Ireland. He's alone now.
Arlo Oh, I'm sorry.
Emily It's OK. My Aunt Cathleen goes to see Grandpa a lot. Aunt Cathleen is my dad's sister. She and my Uncle Tim and my cousins Ella and Ronan live in an old house with a big garden. Ella is 16 and Ronan is 12.

Who is it? Write the name of the person.
Wer ist gemeint? Schreibe den Namen der Person.

1 His partner is a man from Ireland. He's _____.
2 She lives in Ireland. She is Ronan's mum. She's _____.
3 Her mum is Emily's aunt. She lives in Ireland. She's _____.
4 He is Rory's dad. He's _____.
5 He lives in Bristol. He's Emily's mum's partner. He's _____.
6 She has rabbits in her garden. She's Erica's mum. She's _____.

▶ Check

2 WORDS Your family ___ / 7
▶ SB, p. 44, p. 189

a) **Find the right word.**
Finde das richtige Wort.

1 Your dad's brother is your _____.
2 Your aunt's son is your _____.
3 Your dad's dad is your _____.
4 Your mum is your uncle's _____.
5 Your mum's sister is your _____.

b) **Write two more family words.**
Schreibe zwei weitere Begriffe zum Thema Familie.

_____   _____

3 LANGUAGE On the phone ___ / 10
▶ SB, p. 47, p. 178

Sita is on the phone with her Uncle Ravi. Complete their dialogue with *am/is/are* or *'m not/isn't/aren't*.
Sita telefoniert mit ihrem Onkel Ravi. Vervollständige den Dialog mit am/is/are *oder* 'm not/isn't/aren't.

Ravi Hi, Sita. It's Uncle Ravi. How are you? Are you OK?

Sita Yes, I _____. I'm here in the kitchen with Lucky and Sam, our dogs.

Ravi Yes, I can hear them.

Sita Oh. _____ they too loud?

Ravi No, they _____, it's OK.
_____ they hungry?

Sita Yes, they _____. They're always hungry.

Ravi Is your mum there too?

Sita No, she _____. She's at work.

Ravi What? It's the weekend!

Sita I know. She works a lot.

Ravi What about your dad? _____ he at home?

Sita Yes, he _____. But he's busy in the garden.

Ravi Oh, so you're alone. Are you sad about that?

Sita No, I _____. It's OK. Lucky and Sam are here next to me. What about you, Uncle Ravi? _____ you in your flat?

▶ Check

4 LISTENING Can you say the name again?   ___ / 6   ▶ SB, p. 60, p. 168, p. 258

a) Sita talks on the phone with her Uncle Ravi again. Listen and tick (✓) true or false.
Sita telefoniert wieder mit ihrem Onkel Ravi. Höre zu und hake ab: true oder false. (4 Punkte)

	true	false
1 Sita is at home with Lucky.		
2 Uncle Ravi is very busy in his garden.		
3 Sita and Lucky want to go home.		
4 Uncle Ravi can help.		

b) Uncle Ravi's notes are missing some numbers and letters. Listen again and complete the address of the vet.
In Onkel Ravis Notizen fehlen Buchstaben und Zahlen. Höre noch einmal zu und vervollständige die Adresse der Tierärztin. (2 Punkte)

Dr Berry's Vet Clinic
__ __ __ __ C__ __ __ __ o Street

5 WORDS Talking about pets   ___ / 8   ▶ SB, pp. 48–49, p. 190

Complete the sentences with the right animals.
Vervollständige die Sätze mit den richtigen Tieren.

1 I love our two _____. They're so small and quiet.
2 Can I sit on the _____? I'm not scared. They're really big and fast, but so cool too.
3 Jen's green _____ looks mean, but he's really very friendly.
4 My _____ likes to talk. He can say "Hello"!
5 Jumpy, our _____ is messy, but he's so cute.
6 – Ah! There's a _____ under your bed!
   – Oh, don't worry, that's Sid. Are you scared? I can put him in his terrarium.
7 I have a very sweet and clever _____. She can open and close the door. When we walk on the beach, she likes to play and go in the water.
8 It's fun to watch my brother's _____. They swim so fast.

▶ Check

6 LISTENING Olivia's dream room   ___ / 8   ▶ SB, pp. 52–55, p. 190

a) Olivia talks to her friend Arun. Look at the pictures and find some things that are different. Then listen to the conversation. What's her dream room? Tick (✓) room A or B.
Olivia redet mit ihrem Freund Arun. Schaue die Bilder an und finde die Unterschiede. Dann höre dem Gespräch zu. Was ist ihr Traumzimmer? Markiere Zimmer A oder B. (1 Punkt)

b) Listen again and look at the pictures (1–7). What does Olivia talk about? Tick (✓) the numbers.
Höre noch einmal zu und schaue die Bilder an (1–7). Worüber redet Olivia? Markiere die Nummern. (7 Punkte)

1 lamp 2 wardrobe 3 chair 4 table 5 bed 6 sofa 7 shelves

7 LANGUAGE Two rooms   ___ / 5   ▶ SB, p. 52, p. 178

Look again at the two rooms in 6a). What's different? Write sentences with *There is/are (no) …*
Schaue die Zimmer in 6a) noch einmal an. Was ist anders? Schreibe Sätze mit There is/are (no) …

1 cushions: *There are two cushions on the bed in room A.*

2 guitar: _____

3 pictures: _____

4 shelves: _____

5 pens: _____

6 shoes: _____

▶ Check

8 LANGUAGE Questions, questions ___ / 4 ▶ SB, p. 54

Arun has some more questions for Olivia, but they're mixed up. Put the words in the right order.
Arun hat weitere Fragen an Olivia, aber sie sind durcheinander. Setze die Wörter in die richtige Reihenfolge.

1 the dancer / is / the poster / who / on ?

Who is the dancer on the poster?

2 next to / the window / are / the shelves ?

_____

3 your / where / wardrobe / is ?

_____

4 bed / is / your / the door / near ?

_____

5 is / the shelves / on / what / ?

_____

9 WORDS Arun's house ___ / 7 ▶ SB, p. 51

Write the names of the places in Arun's house (1–7). The words are in the box.
Schreibe die Bezeichnungen der Orte in Aruns Haus (1–7). Die Wörter sind im Kasten.

1 _____

2 _____

3 _____

4 _____

5 _____

6 _____

7 _____

bathroom • bedroom • dining room • garden • hall • kitchen • living room

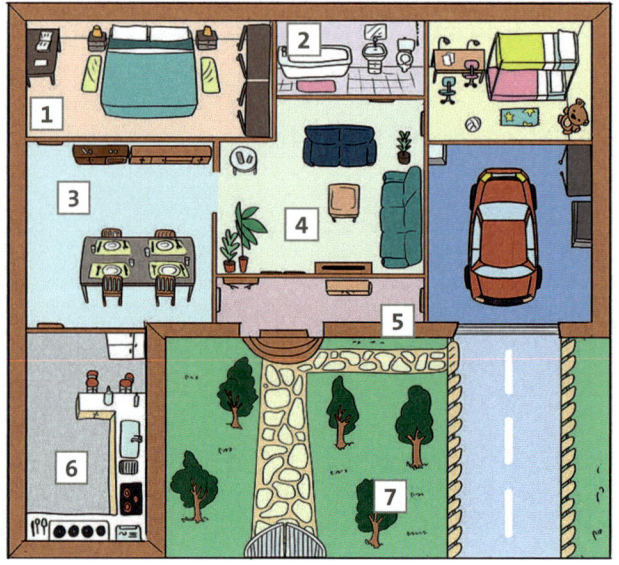

▶ Check

10 WRITING Email to a friend ____ / 15   ▶ More help, p. 74   ▶ SB, p. 51, pp. 215–217

Arun gets an email from his penfriend Mara. She tells him about her flat. She wants to know more about his home. Write Arun's email and describe his house (see 9, page 20).

Arun bekommt eine E-Mail von seiner Brieffreundin Mara. Sie erzählt ihm von ihrer Wohnung. Sie will mehr über sein Zuhause wissen. Schreibe Aruns E-Mail und beschreibe sein Haus (siehe 9, Seite 20).

Answer these questions:
– What are the rooms like? (big, small, nice, etc.)
– Where is the kitchen? (next to / …)
– Where is your room?
– What do you like?

Hi Mara,

Thanks for your email! I can tell you about my home. _____

My house is _____

There is _____

And there are _____

_____

_____

I really like _____

That's my house!
Write back soon!
Arun

Bereich	Aufgabe	erreichte Punktzahl	🤩	😎	🤔	😭
listening	4 6	____ / 6 ____ / 8 } ____ / 14	14–13	12–10	9–7	6–0
reading	1	____ / 6	6	5–4	3	2–0
words	2 5 9	____ / 7 ____ / 8 } ____ / 22 ____ / 7	22–20	19–16	15–11	10–0
language	3 7 8	____ / 10 ____ / 5 } ____ / 19 ____ / 4	19–17	16–14	13–10	9–0
writing	10	____ / 15	15–14	13–11	10–8	7–0
Gesamt		____ / 76	76–69	68–53	52–38	37–0

Unit 3
My day

1 LISTENING School days _____ / 10 ▶ SB, p. 77

🔊 07

a) Daniel, Jess, Su and Milo talk about their daily routines. Read the questions and listen for the answers. Match the letters (A–D) with the right answer.
Daniel, Jess, Su und Milo reden über ihren normalen Tagesablauf. Lies die Fragen und achte beim Hören auf die Antworten. Schreibe die Buchstaben (A–D) zur richtigen Antwort. (4 Punkte)

How do they go to school?

1 ___ takes the bus to school.

2 ___ goes to school by car.

3 ___ walks to school.

4 ___ cycles to school.

Daniel

Jess

Su

Milo

b) Listen again. True or false? Tick (✓).
Höre noch einmal zu. Richtig oder falsch? Markiere (✓). (6 Punkte)

		true	false
1	After school Daniel likes to play guitar.		
2	Daniel's mum comes home from work at five p.m.		
3	Jess's home is near her school.		
4	Su gets up after her sister.		
5	Su meets her friend at the bus stop at seven fifteen.		
6	Milo is in the hockey club.		

▶ Check

2 WORDS Time to go ____ / 8

▶ SB, p. 78, p. 191

a) **Underline the correct time.**
Unterstreiche die korrekte Uhrzeit.

1. What's the time? – It's twelve twenty-four / twelve thirty-four – Thanks.
2. Where's the bus? It always comes at six forty / seven forty.
3. We have our morning break at ten fifty / ten fifteen.
4. Don't forget, the game starts at four o'clock / six o'clock.

b) **Underline the correct digital time.** *Unterstreiche die korrekte digitale Zeit.*

5. The assembly rarely ends at nine fifty. 19:15 / 9:50
6. They take the bus home after school at three twenty-five. 3:45 / 3:25
7. On Saturdays I go running at ten thirty in the morning. 10:30 / 10:13
8. At our school, lunchtime is at twelve forty-five. 12:45 / 11:45

3 LANGUAGE On Saturday ____ / 12

▶ SB, p. 80, p. 179

Marla tells a classmate about her Saturdays. Complete her sentences with the right verbs and verb forms.
Marla erzählt von ihren Samstagen. Vervollständige ihre Sätze mit den richtigen Verben und den richtigen Verbformen.

1. | eat • get • go • take |

On Saturday I _____ up at about nine thirty. After I _____ breakfast, I'm ready for the day. I often _____ cycling with my friend Josh. Our favourite bike ride _____ 30 minutes. Cycling is great!

2. | do • eat • listen • read |

My parents _____ breakfast very late. My mum _____ art in the morning. She's very good at it. My dad often _____ to music or he _____ a book.

3. | go • eat • walk • play |

We always _____ lunch at about one p.m. and later we _____ to the beach. My sister and my dad often _____ football and my mum and I _____ on the beach. It's nice!

▶ Check

4 Reading It's not Brighton ___ / 8

▶ SB, p. 82, p. 219–224

Carla, Tim and Zola are Brighton school friends, but now Zola lives in Glasgow. They do a video call. Read their dialogue.
Carla, Tim and Zola sind Schulfreunde aus Brighton, aber jetzt wohnt Zola in Glasgow. Sie machen einen Videoanruf. Lies ihren Dialog.

Carla Is Glasgow nice, Zola?
Zola Yes, it is. It's OK, but it's not Brighton.
Tim What about your new school? Are the students and teachers friendly?
Zola Yes, they're very helpful. I'm lucky. And I meet people in the canteen and I do activities after school.
Carla That's clever. Then you can make friends fast. Are you in a school club?
Zola Yes, I'm in the dance club. We meet on Tuesdays after school.
Tim Oh wow! Is that fun?
Zola It's so much fun. We do hip-hop and street dancing.
Tim Cool! I often dance to hip-hop music at the weekends with Yusef and Ina.
Zola Yes, I remember. You're good at it, Tim. I'm not, but I really like dancing.

Carla Is your school near your home?
Zola No, not really. That's a problem. Glasgow is very big, and I go to school by bus. The journey often takes 45 minutes. It's loud and stressful[1].
Tim Oh no. That's not good.
Carla I'm sorry, Zola. Hey guys, it's eight twenty now and my favourite TV show starts in five minutes. Let's do this again.
Zola Good idea! What about on Sunday at four thirty?
Tim Sorry, I'm busy on Sunday. Are you all free on Saturday evening?
Zola What time?
Tim Seven forty-five?
Zola Yes, I'm free.
Carla Yeah, OK!
Tim Great!

Complete the sentences.
Vervollständige die Sätze. (8 Punkte)

1 In school activities Zola can _____.
2 Zola goes dancing on _____.
3 Zola's journey to school takes _____.
4 The friends want to meet again on _____.
5 Zola says the students and teachers are _____.
6 Tim is good at _____.
7 In five minutes Carla's _____ is starting.
8 Tim can't talk on Sunday because he's _____.

▶ Check

---

[1] **stressfull** *anstrengend, stressig*

5 LANGUAGE Weekend activities ____ / 5   ▶ SB, p. 83, p. 179

Write what they do at the weekend. Use the simple present and the words in the box.
Schreibe, was sie am Wochenende tun. Benutze das simple present und die Wörter im Kasten.

always, often, sometimes, rarely, never
Diese Wörter geben an, **wie häufig** man etwas tut. Diese Häufigkeitsadverbien stehen meist zwischen dem Subjekt und dem Verb:
On Saturday   I   **often**   go   swimming.
At the weekend my parents **sometimes**   play   music.

teeth • homework • swimming • video games • ~~table tennis~~ • TV

1 Mike and his dad
   often play table tennis.

2 Arav sometimes
   _____

3 I always
   _____

4 Jenna rarely
   _____

5 Alex and I often
   _____

6 Mum never
   _____

6 WORDS Feelings ____ / 6   ▶ SB, pp. 88–90

Write the correct word for each emoji. *Schreibe das richtige Wort für jedes Emoji.*

1

s __ d

2

h __ __ __ y

3

su __ __ __ __ __ d

4

a __ __ __ y

5

so __ __ y

6

t __ __ __ d

▶ Check

twenty-five **25**

3

7 WRITING My Saturday ____ / 15   ▶ More help, p. 75   ▶ SB, pp. 79–80

Write about a normal Saturday for you at home. Write what you and your family do and when you do it. You can use words or phrases from the two boxes. Write six sentences or more. *Schreibe über einen normalen Samstag bei dir zu Hause. Schreibe, was du und deine Familie macht und wann ihr es macht. Du kannst die Wörter und Satzteile aus den Kästen benutzen. Schreibe sechs oder mehr Sätze.*

💡 Bei dieser Aufgabe sollst du über dich und deine Familie schreiben.
Schreibe, **wann** **wer** **was** tut.
Example: After that   my dad   reads the newspaper.
           Then   I   have lunch.
Du kannst auch sagen,   My brother **often/always/sometimes**
wie häufig jemand etwas tut.   goes running.

| in the morning/afternoon/evening • at .. o'clock • at the weekend • on Saturday • before/after ... • then | get up • have a shower • get dressed • eat/have/make breakfast/lunch/dinner • tidy up • meet with ... • play games/sport • go cycling/skateboarding/swimming/shopping/... • do art/street dancing... • watch TV / a film • read a book/magazine/newspaper • text with friends • go to bed at ... |

On Saturday I get up at _____. I have a _____, then I _____

_____. After that I _____

_____

_____

We have lunch at _____. Sometimes I eat _____

In the afternoon, _____

_____

_____

After dinner, _____

_____

_____

▶ Check

8 SKILLS **Word play** ____ / 11 ▶ SB, p. 92, p. 169

a) **Find the odd word out. Circle it.**
   Finde das Wort, das nicht in die Reihe passt. Kreise es ein.

   Example: lunch – (snack) – breakfast – dinner

   1 often – sometimes – weekend – always
   2 teacher – get up – shower – brush my teeth
   3 breakfast – parkour – swimming – cycling
   4 angry – happy – history – tired
   5 bike – tree – bus – car
   6 book – pencil – newspaper – magazine
   7 football – sofa – lamp – chair

b) **Add one or more words to make a word field.**
   Füge ein Wort hinzu, um ein Wortfeld zu bilden.

   Example: afternoon – evening – morning – night

   8 science, geography, computing, _____
   9 tired, hungry, surprised, _____
   10 tennis, basketball, swimming, _____
   11 kitchen, bathroom, dining room, _____

Bereich	Aufgabe	erreichte Punktzahl	🤩	😎	🤔	😭
listening	1	___ / 10	10–9	8–7	6–5	4–0
words	2 6	___ / 8 ___ / 6 ___ / 14	14–13	12–10	9–7	6–0
language	3 5	___ / 12 ___ / 5 ___ / 17	17–16	15–12	11–9	8–0
reading	4	___ / 8	8–7	6	5–4	3–0
writing	7	___ / 15	15–14	13–11	10–8	7–0
skills	8	___ / 11	11–10	9–8	7–6	5–0
Gesamt		___ / 75	75–68	67–53	52–38	37–0

▶ Check

BASIC

lighthouse 1

Klassenarbeitstrainer
Lösungen

Lösungen

Hello! Nice to meet you

1 LISTENING Four kids

Hörtext

Magda Hi! I'm Magda and I'm twelve. I'm from London, England. My hobby is listening to music, but I don't like dancing. My favourite colour is red.

Amir Hello, I'm Amir and I'm ten years old. I'm from England too, but I'm from Plymouth. I don't like dancing but I like books. My favourite colour is orange.

Ben Hi, I'm Ben. I'm twelve and I'm from Germany. My hobby is swimming and I like TV. My favourite colour is blue.

Tanya Hello! I'm Tanya and I'm from Ireland. I'm eleven years old. My favourite colour is green. I don't like TV, but I like music.

Alle Lösungen aus diesem Heft findest du auch in deiner Cornelsen Lernen App

a) 2 b, e • 3 f • 4 c

b)

Amir — (orange)/ red / pink

Ben — yellow / green /(blue)

Tanya — white /(green)/ blue

2 WORDS What about you?
1. sport; swimming
2. animal; horse
3. thing; bike
4. hobby; taking photos
5. colour; red

3 WORDS Word pairs
1. bad – good
2. close – open
3. big – small
4. right – wrong
5. old – new

4 WORDS Word spiral

1 white
2 green
3 red
4 black
5 orange
6 brown

Wörter lernen mit *Vocabulary*
Alle neue Wörter und Wendungen des Schulbuches findest du im *Vocabulary*, Schulbuch S. 213–253.

- Lies dir zunächst das englische Wort laut vor
- Lies dann die deutsche Übersetzung und die Beispiele und Hinweise in der rechten Spalte.
- Schreibe das englische Wort auf und präge dir so die Schreibweise ein.
- Wiederhole diese Schritte mehrfach hintereinander, um die Wörter gut zu merken. Wechsle dabei auch die Leserichtung: Beginne mit der deutschen Übersetzung, sage dann das englische Wort.
- Teste dich nun selbst: Decke die deutsche Übersetzung ab, lies das englische Wort. Weißt du noch, was es auf Deutsch bedeutet? Kannst du auch englische Beispiele nennen?
- Du kannst auch jemand bitten dich abzufragen.

5 WORDS Animals

1 monkey • 2 lion • 3 dogs • 4 elephant • 5 snakes • 6 fish

6 READING I like it

Hannah	Hello! How are you?
Dev	Oh, hi! I'm fine.
Hannah	I'm Hannah. What's your **name**?
Dev	I'm Dev. Nice to **meet** you, Hannah.
Hannah	I like your (1) **hat**.
Dev	Thanks.
Hannah	It's blue. That's my favourite **colour**.
Dev	Yes, blue is nice.
Dev	Oh! Look out! There's a big (2) **dog**!
Hannah	It's OK. That's Minnie. She's nice.
Dev	She's big and, oh no, she's in my (3) **bag**.
Hannah	Minnie …
Dev	Hey, that's my (4) **sandwich**!
Hannah	Minnie, no! Sorry, she's hungry.
Dev	I don't like dogs.
Hannah	Oh. What's your favourite **animal**?
Dev	I like (5) **cats**. They're small and quiet.
Hannah	Sorry. Let's go, Minnie. Nice to meet you, Dev! Bye!

Lösungen

Unit 1 My new school

1 LISTENING A day at school
Hörtexte

02
Josh	Hi, Vera.
Vera	Oh, hi, Josh! How are you?
Josh	Fine, thanks. Am I late?
Vera	No, you're early.
Josh	That's good. It's a busy day.
Vera	Hey, I like your pencil case. It's blue – my favourite colour!
Josh	Yeah, I like blue too. Oh! Mrs Martin is here.
Mrs Martin	OK, quiet please. Sit down please and open your books to page 8.
Josh	Right. Where's my maths book? Ah, here it is.
Vera	Maths? This isn't maths, Josh. This is geography!
Josh	Heh? Oh, yeah! Geography. I'm very tired today.

03
Maya	Hello, Mr Brown.
Mr Brown	Oh, hello Maya.
Maya	Can you help me?
Mr Brown	Yes. What is it?
Maya	Where is the computer room? Is it here?
Mr Brown	No, this is the art room, the computer room is in room 11.
Maya	Oh, OK. … Erm, where is room 11?
Mr Brown	That's in building 1, near the canteen.
Maya	It's not here in building 2? *(sighs)* This is a big school!
Mr Brown	Yes, it is. Now go, Maya. Don't be late.
Maya	OK, thanks!

04
Naveed	Hello. Can I sit here?
Erin	Hi! Yes, you can.
Naveed	My name's Naveed. What's your name?
Erin	I'm Erin.
Naveed	Nice to meet you, Erin. I'm happy it's lunch! I'm hungry!
Erin	The food isn't bad in here today.
Naveed	I have my lunch in my bag. *(to himself)* Where is it? Ah, here!
Erin	A sandwich? I don't like sandwiches.
Naveed	My dad's sandwiches are great. I love them.
Erin	That's cool.

a) Josh: d • Maya: c • Naveed: b
b)

	right	wrong
1 Josh is late for his class.		✓
2 Josh has the wrong book.	✓	
3 The computer room is in room 10.		✓
4 Maya's school is big.	✓	
5 The lunch food is good today.	✓	
6 Naveed has a sandwich from his mum.		✓

2 WORDS What can you see?
1 a pencil case • 2 a rubber • 3 a glue stick • 4 a pencil sharpener • 5 an exercise book • 6 a pen • 7 an orange • 8 a ruler • 9 an apple • 10 an English book

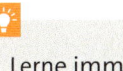

Lerne immer nur fünf bis zehn Wöter auf einmal.

3 WORDS History lesson

Ms Lopez	Good morning, students. Quiet, please.
Beth	**Can** I open the window, please?
Ms Lopez	Yes, you can. Now find your history **book** and …
Maya	Sorry I'm late, Ms Lopez.
Ms Lopez	OK, Maya, but don't **be** late again. Now listen, class. **Open** your book at page …
Emilia	Ms Lopez, can **I go** to the toilet, please?
Ms Lopez	Yes, you can.
Maya	What page **is** it, Sophie?
Sophie	I don't know.
Ms Lopez	**Don't** talk! Let's start now. It's page 12. Read the text. Then **answer** the questions.
Sophie	This is hard. Can you **help** me?
Ms Lopez	Yes, I can.

4 LANGUAGE My timetable

Hi Esme,
My timetable this year isn't bad. I'm lucky. Design is my favourite subject. **It**'s very cool. I have music and art too. My teachers aren't bad. **They**'re friendly. Mr Williams is my music teacher. **He** can sing and play the guitar. I think that's really cool. Suriya is in my class too. Do **you** remember Suriya? **She**'s great. After music, Suriya and I go to the canteen. **We** always see Jonas and Dev there. We like them. **They**'re nice. Yeah, my school is OK. How are **you**? How is your timetable?
Bye, Santi

Lösungen

5 LANGUAGE Three students

1. Hi, I'm David. My school **is** great. It **isn't** big. I like that. Computing and sport **are** my favourite classes. They**'re** on Thursday.
2. Hi, I'm Kezia. **I'm not** from Brighton. Brighton **is** new for me. It**'s** nice here. The kids at school **aren't** mean. They **are** really friendly.
3. Hello, I'm Annie. Charlie and Ahmad **are** my school friends. We**'re** in the same history class. History **isn't** my favourite subject, but it**'s** fun with Charlie and Ahmad.

6 READING At Winford School

	Kezia	Nick	Annie	David
1 I have music on Friday morning.		✓		
2 After lunch on Monday I go to the sports hall.				✓
3 I have French after lunch on Wednesday.			✓	
4 I like Tuesdays because I have music and art.	✓			
5 My class teacher is my science teacher too.			✓	
6 My two favourite lessons are on Monday.		✓		

7 LANGUAGE What's Wrong?

1. It isn't swimming. It's football.
2. She isn't ten. She is nine.
3. Erin: No, you're not late. You're on time.
4. They aren't in the computer room. They're in the canteen.
5. No, I'm not from Brighton. I'm from [Ort, aus dem du kommst].

8 WORDS School topics

S	T	U	D	E	N	T	P	C
T	O	L	C	K	D	V	H	L
V	E	L	O	D	S	S	E	A
G	N	A	G	M	A	T	H	S
P	E	N	C	I	L	S	I	S
F	C	O	V	H	W	J	O	R
A	F	B	G	I	E	M	L	O
U	Q	E	R	R	N	R	G	O
B	I	N	P	U	A	G	L	M
M	K	W	L	L	Z	P	L	M
C	A	N	T	E	E	N	H	O
O	S	C	H	R	V	F	E	Y

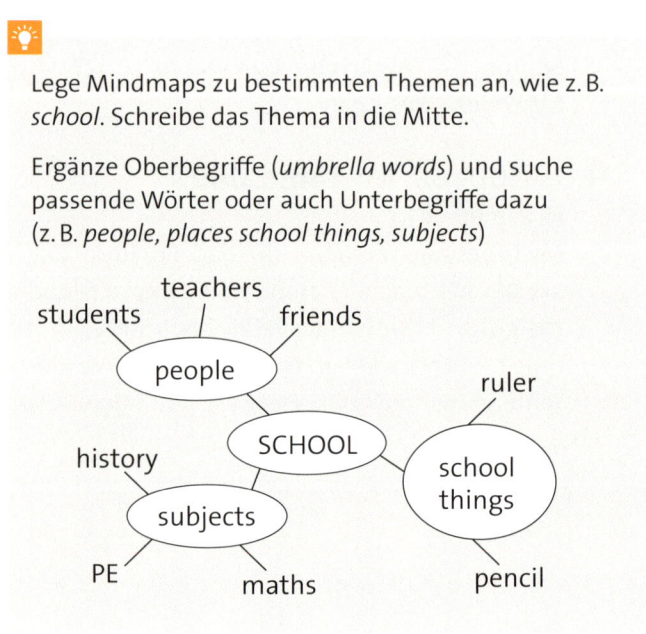

Lege Mindmaps zu bestimmten Themen an, wie z. B. *school*. Schreibe das Thema in die Mitte.

Ergänze Oberbegriffe (*umbrella words*) und suche passende Wörter oder auch Unterbegriffe dazu (z. B. *people, places school things, subjects*)

9 Writing An email to a friend

Benutze die Checkliste um zu kontrollieren, ob du die Aufgabe erfüllt hast. Hast du etwas über die folgenden Themen geschrieben? Gib dir drei Punkte für jedes Thema, das du erwähnt hast.

		✓
your school and class	The name of my school is … I'm in class …	
your teachers	My (favourite) teacher is … She/He is (not) OK/nice/great/helpful/…. She/He is my history/PE/maths/… teacher.	
the kids at school	The kids at my school are/aren't …	
your timetable and favourite subject	My timetable is very … My favourite lesson/subject is …	
your friends at school	My school friends are … and … … in my music class / the same class / a different class.	
	Total: _____ / 15	

(*Lösungsbeispiel*)

Hi Jamie,

Today I want to write to you about my school. The name of my school is Rothenburg-Schule. I'm in class 7B and my teacher is Ms Weiss. My favourite teacher is Mr Lehmann. He's my English teacher. The kids at my school aren't mean. They're really nice. My timetable is very good. I have English on Monday, Wednesday and Thursday. My favourite lesson is art. That's lesson 5 on Tuesday. My friends at school are Ali, Nola, Senna and Jakob.

That's my school!

Bye,

Billie

> In einem Vokabelordner (Vocab file) kannst du Wörter sammeln und in Listen, Mindmaps und Tabellen ordnen.
>
> Dadurch kannst du sie nicht nur besser lernen und behalten, sondern auch noch später nuzten, z. B. wenn du über ein Thema sprechen oder schreiben möchtest.

Unit 2 My family and home

1 READING My family
1 Steve • 2 Aunt Cathleen • 3 Ella • 4 Grandpa Liam • 5 Enrico • 6 Grandma Lynn

2 WORDS Your family
a) 1 uncle • 2 cousin • 3 grandpa • 4 sister • 5 aunt

b) *(Lösungsbeispiel)*
mum, dad, grandma, brother, …

3 LANGUAGE On the phone

Ravi	Hi, Sita. It's Uncle Ravi. How are you? Are you OK?
Sita	Yes, I **am.** I'm here in the kitchen with Lucky and Sam, our dogs.
Ravi	Yes, I can hear them.
Sita	Oh. **Are** they too loud?
Ravi	No, they **aren't.** Well, maybe. **Are** they hungry?
Sita	Yes, they **are.** They're always hungry.
Ravi	Is your mum there too?
Sita	No, she **isn't.** She's at work.
Ravi	What about your dad? **Is** he at home?
Sita	Yes, he **is.** But he's busy in the garden.
Ravi	Oh, so you're alone. Are you sad about that?
Sita	No, I**'m not,** It's OK. Lucky and Sam are here next to me. What about you, Uncle Ravi? **Are** you in your flat?

4 LISTENING Can you say the name again?
Hörtext

🔊 05

Ravi	Hello?
Sita	Hi, Uncle Ravi!
Ravi	Sita? Is that you?
Sita	Yes, it is.
Ravi	Where are you? Are you at home?
Sita	No, I'm not. I'm at the vet with Lucky.
Ravi	Oh! Is Lucky OK?
Sita	Yes, he is now. He's very quiet, but he's fine.
Ravi	Lucky is a good dog. And you're a good friend, Sita.
Sita	Thanks, Uncle Ravi. I have a question for you. Are you busy now?
Ravi	Now? Not really. I'm in the garden behind the house. Can I help you and Lucky?
Sita	The problem is, we want to go home, but Mum is at work and Dad can't come now.
Ravi	Oh, I see. I can come and get you in my car.
Sita	Do you really have time?

Ravi	Yes, yes.	
Sita	Oh, thank you, Uncle Ravi!	
Ravi	It's no problem. What's the name of the vet?	
Sita	It's Dr. Berry's Vet Clinic.	
Ravi	Oh. I can't hear you very well. Can you spell the name?	
Sita	Yes. It's B–e–r–r–y. Dr. Berry.	
Ravi	OK. And what's the address?	
Sita	It's sixteen-oh-five, that's one-six-oh-five Calico Street.	
Ravi	Can you say that again, please?	
Sita	Sixteen-oh-five Calico Street. I can spell it for you. It's c–a–l–i–c–o.	
Ravi	Calico Street. OK. And what's the number?	
Sita	It's one-six-oh-five.	
Ravi	OK. I can be there in ten minutes.	
Sita	Great! Let's meet in front of the clinic, next to the big doors.	
Ravi	Right. See you soon!	
Sita	Thanks. Bye!	

a)

	true	false
1 Sita is at home with Lucky.		✓
2 Uncle Ravi is very busy in the garden.		✓
3 Sita and Lucky want to go home.	✓	
4 Uncle Ravi can help.	✓	

b)

> *Dr Berry's Vet Clinic*
> *1 6 7 5 C a l i c o Street*

5 Words Talking about pets
1 hamsters • 2 horse • 3 lizard • 4 parrot • 5 rabbit • 6 snake • 7 dog • 8 fish

6 Listening Olivia's dream room
Hörtext

Olivia	… now I want to tell you about my dream room, Arun.
Arun	Ooh, yes. What's it like?
Olivia	In my dream room the walls are yellow, and the bed is really nice with blue cushions. There are some shelves near the bed and lots of my things are on the shelves.
Arun	Hm. OK. Is there a window in this dream room?
Olivia	Oh yes. The window is on the other wall and my desk is in front of it. I can sit on my chair and look out the window.
Arun	Nice. I like that. Where's your computer?
Olivia	There is no computer.
Arun	Oh, OK. What's on your desk then?

Lösungen

Olivia My pet robot, Hal, is on my desk.
Arun Ah, Hal. Cool. And … what about a lamp?
Olivia My dream room has a lamp on a small table next to my bed and there's another lamp on my desk.
Arun That's good. Are there pictures on the walls?
Olivia Yes – there's a poster of my favourite dancer.
And here's my favourite thing: you can open a door and there's a big balcony with a table and two chairs.
Arun Wow. That's a cool room!

a) Room B

b)

1 ✓ lamp 2 ☐ wardrobe 3 ✓ chair 4 ✓ table 5 ✓ bed 6 ☐ sofa 7 ✓ shelves

7 LANGUAGE Two rooms
(*Lösungsbeispiel*)
2 There is a guitar (next to the bed) in room A. / There is no guitar (next to the bed) in room B.
3 There are three pictures (on the wall) in room B. / There is one picture (on the wall) in room A.
4 There are books on the shelves in room B. / There are no books on the shelves in room A.
5 There are pens (on the desk) in room B. / There are no pens (on the desk) in room A.
6 There are shoes (under the desk) in room B. / There are no shoes (under the desk) in room A.

8 LANGUAGE Questions, questions
2 Are the shelves next to the window?
3 Where is your wardrobe?
4 Is your bed near the door? / Is the door near your bed?
5 What is on the shelves?

9 WORDS Arun's house
1 bedroom • 2 bathroom • 3 dining room • 4 living room • 5 hall • 6 kitchen • 7 garden

10 Writing Email to a friend

Benutze die Checkliste um zu kontrollieren, ob du die Aufgabe erfüllt hast. Hast du etwas über die folgenden Themen geschrieben? Gib dir drei Punkte für jeden Punkt, den du erfüllt hast.

		✓
What are the rooms like?	My room / the kitchen / the living room / ... is big/different/messy/modern/nice/old/small/tidy. There's a big/small/... living room / bathroom / dining room.	
Where is the kitchen?	The kitchen is in front of the dining room / next to the garden.	
Where is your room?	My room is next to the bathroom / next to the living room.	
What do you like?	I really like ... It's big/different/great/nice/tidy	
Did you write 6 or more sentences?		
	Total: _____ / 15	

(*Lösungsbeispiel*)

Hi Mara,

Thanks for your email! I can tell you about my home. I live in a house with my family. My house is very nice. There is a hall, a kitchen, a dining room, a living room, and a bathroom. The hall is small, but the kitchen, dining room and living room are big. And there are two bedrooms. The bedrooms are not too small and not too big. The garden is in front of the house. It's very tidy and there are lots of trees. The kitchen is in front of the dining room. My room is next to the living room and the bathroom. I really like my bedroom, it's tidy. That's my house!

Write back soon!

Arun

> **!**
>
> Mit *there is* (= *there's*) oder *there are* sagst du, dass etwas vorhanden ist.
>
> Im Deutschen heißt es meist:
> Es gibt ...
> Da sind ...
> Es stehen ...
> Da liegen ...

Lösungen

Unit 3 My day

1 LISTENING School days
Hörtext

🔊 07

A: Hi, I'm **Daniel**. I get up at 6:30 a.m. My brother and I have breakfast and then our mum takes us to school by car. After school my brother has football training and I often play guitar. On Wednesdays I do the shopping because my mum works and she can't do it. She comes home at about 7 p.m. and makes dinner for us. That's our day!

B: Hi, my name is **Jess**. I always get up at 7 o'clock and have a shower. After breakfast I walk to school. It's only ten minutes from our house. That's really cool. After school I often do art with my best friend. I'm good at it, but she's really good. Sometimes I have dinner alone when my parents are too busy. It's not great, but it's OK.

C: Hello, I'm **Su**. I get up early because it's a long journey from my home to school. I get up at 6 o'clock. I get dressed really fast, then I have more time for breakfast. My sister gets up later. She goes to a different school. I meet my friend Mina at the bus stop at 7:15 and we take the bus. After school I go to swim training. I'm always tired after that.

D: Hi guys, I'm **Milo**. I get up at 7:20. My school is only ten minutes from our home and I go by bike. My friends say I'm lucky. At school I'm in the cricket club, so in the afternoon I often play cricket. It's great. After cricket I go home by bike and we have dinner at about 6:30 p.m.

a)
1 __C__ takes the bus to school
2 __A__ goes to school by car.
3 __B__ walks to school.
4 __D__ cycles to school.

b)

	true	false
1 After school Daniel likes to play guitar.	✓	
2 Daniel's mum comes home from work at five p.m.		✓
3 Jess's home is near her school.	✓	
4 Su gets up after her sister.		✓
5 Su meets her friend at the bus stop at seven fifteen.	✓	
6 Milo is in the hockey club.		✓

2 Words Time to go
1 Twelve twenty-four • 2 Seven forty • 3 ten fifteen • 4 four o'clock
5 9:50 • 6 3:25 • 7 10:30 • 8 12:45

3 Language On Saturday
1 On Saturday I **get** up at about nine thirty. After I **eat** breakfast, I'm ready for the day. I often **go** cycling with my friend Josh. His house isn't far. Our favourite bike ride **takes** about 30 minutes. Cycling is great!
2 My parents **eat** breakfast very late. My mum **does** art in the morning. She's very good at it. My dad often **listens** to music or he **reads** a book.
3 We always **eat** lunch at about one p.m. and later we **go** to the beach. We **ride** our bikes because it's too far to walk. My sister and my dad often **play** football and my mum and I **walk** on the beach.

4 Reading It's not Brighton
1 make friends
2 Tuesdays
3 45 minutes
4 Saturday (evening)
5 friendly / helpful
6 hip-hop (dancing)
7 favourite TV show
8 busy

5 Language Weekend activities
2 Aarav sometimes goes swimming.
3 I always brush my teeth.
4 Jenna rarely does homework.
5 Alex and I often watch TV.
6 Mum never plays video games.

> Anders als im Deutschen stehen die Häufigkeitsadverbien (*always, often, sometimes, rarely, never*) im Englischen meist direkt vor dem Hauptverb.
> Toni *often plays* volleyball.
> Toni spielt oft Volleyball.

6 Words Feelings

1   s _a_ d

2  h _a_ _p_ _p_ y

3  su _r_ _p_ _r_ _i_ _s_ _e_ d

4   a _n_ _g_ _r_ y

5   so _r_ _r_ y

6  t _i_ _r_ _e_ d

Lösungen

7 WRITING My Saturday

Benutze die Checkliste um zu kontrollieren, ob du die Aufgabe erfüllt hast. Gib dir drei Punkte für jede Frage, die du mit „ja" beantwortest. Wenn du die Aufgabe nur zum Teil erfüllt hast, gib dir zwei Punkte.

Does your text have...		ja = 3 Punkte zum Teil = 2 Punkte
six (or more) verbs?	get up • have a shower • get dressed • tidy up • eat/have/make ... for breakfast/lunch/dinner • meet with ... • text with friends • watch TV / a film • go cycling/swimming/shopping/... • play games/sport/music • do art/coding/yoga/... • read a book/magazine/newspaper • go to bed at...	
two (or more) words for when you do something?	at ... o'clock • at the weekend • before/after ... • then • in the morning/afternoon/evening • on Saturday I do art *in the morning*. *Then* mum and I go shopping.	
two (or more) words for how often you do something?	always • often • sometimes • never I *never* get up before 9 a.m. I *often* play badminton in the afternoon.	
two (or more) people in your family?	My *sister* plays football in the afternoon. My *parents* make lunch for my *grandma*. My *stepdad* and I often take *our dog* to the park.	
six (or more) sentences?		
		Total: _____ / 15

(Lösungsbeispiel)
On Saturday I get up at eight or eigh-thirty a.m. I have a shower and, then I have breakfast. After that I help my parents in the garden. That often takes an hour. Then I text my friends. Sometimes I play with our dog, Nero. He's a lot of fun. We have lunch at 12:30. Sometimes I eat a sandwhich. In the afternoon, I meet with my friends and we play football or go skateboarding. We always have dinner at seven p.m. on Saturday. My mum is a really good cook. After dinner, I like watching TV with my parents or I read a book. I go to bed at about 10 o'clock.

8 SKILLS Word play

a) 1 weekend (not a word for saying how often you do something)
2 teacher (not a verb)
3 breakfast (not a sport)
4 history (not a feeling)
5 tree (not something you can ride to school)
6 pencil (not something you can read)
7 football (no furniture)

> In den Wordbanks (Schulbuch, S. 194–204) findest du viele nützliche Wörter, Sätze und Ausdrücke zu bestimmten Themen wie z. B. Schule, Tiere oder Freizeitaktivitäten.

b) *(Lösungsbeispiele)*
1 science, geography, computing: english • PE • art • maths • ...
2 tired, hungry, surprised: sad • angry • clever • happy • ...
3 tennis, basketball, swimming: football • skateboarding • running • table tennis • ...
4 kitchen, bathroom, dining room: bedroom • living room • garden • hallway • ...

Unit 4 Where I live

1 LISTENING It's their first time here
🔊 08

Hörtext

Alma	Hm. Do they know Brighton very well?
Navid	No, they don't. This is their first time here.
Alma	Then you can take them to Brighton Palace Pier.
Navid	Yes, we want to go there on Saturday. Then we want to go swimming at the beach if the weather is warm and sunny.
Alma	That's a good plan. Do they have hobbies or favourite activities?
Navid	Hm. My cousin Rohan doesn't do a lot of sport activities, but he likes art.
Alma	The Brighton Museum has lots of cool art. I sometimes go there. It's nice.
Navid	That's a good idea. Where is the museum?
Alma	It's in Church Street, near Victoria Gardens.
Navid	Ah, I remember now.
Alma	Yes! Do your cousins like shopping?
Navid	Yes, they do. ... I think. I mean, Rohan loves buying things. My other cousin, Mina, doesn't go shopping very much.
Alma	There's the big shopping centre at Churchill Square. Rohan can go shopping and you and Mina can sit in a cafe there.
Navid	Hey, you're right! Is there a fish and chips shop at Churchill Square?
Alma	No, there isn't. Do you know McGarvey's?
Navid	McGarvey's? No, I don't. What is that?
Alma	It's a fish and chips shop. It's near the pier. They have really good fish and chips. And you can sit outside if it's not rainy.
Navid	Where do you get all these great ideas, Alma?
Alma	I don't know. I don't really go out very much.
Navid	You can come with us, Alma!
Alma	Oh. OK!

a) A 4 • B 1 • C 5 • D 2 • E 3

b) 1 sunny
    2 mueseum / Brighton Museum
    3 go shopping
    4 near
    5 outside, rainy

2 Words In town

1 dirty
2 cinema
3 swap
4 ice rink
5 marina
6 neighbourhood
7 stadium
8 village

A There are lots of boats there.
B It's a place to go skating.
C It's too small to be a city or a town.
D It's a place where you can watch a football game.
E When something isn't clean.
F When you give something to somebody and take something different.
G It's a place where you can watch a film.
H The place where you and your neighbours live.

1 E • 2 G • 3 F • 4 B • 5 A • 6 H • 7 D • 8 C

3 Language New in town

a) 1 **Do** you …? – Yes, I **do**.
2 **Does** the …? – Yes, it **does**.
3 **Do** the buses …? – Yes, they **do**.
4 **Does** the town …? – No, it **doesn't**.
5 **Do** you have …? – No, I **don't**.

b) 1 **When** …? – At 8 o'clock.
2 **Where** …? – The park.
3 **How** often …? – Every weekend!
4 **What** time …? – At 7:45.
5 **Why** …? – Because…

4 Reading Where am I?

a) 1 … cinema
2 … at the skatepark
3 … at the shopping centre

b)

		true	false
1	Where Iris is, people like to go in the evening.	✓	
2	Aisha is at a fun place that costs money.		✓
3	It's really full, where Aisha is.		✓
4	Max is there to shop for clothes.	✓	
5	Where Max is, not everybody wants to shop.	✓	

5 LANGUAGE **Neighbours**

a) 1 I often cycle to school, but **I don't** take my bike when it's windy. It's too hard to ride!
2 Sandy and Leo **don't** need sunny weather to go windsurfing. When it's grey and cloudy outside, that **doesn't** stop them!
3 Brighton **doesn't** often get hot in May, but today it's 26 degrees. I **don't** like it!
4 The Brighton Pier **doesn't** close when it's cold and snowy. It stays open in all weather.
5 Most people **don't** go out when it's rainy, but I like walking on the beach.

b) My friend Zofia doesn't live (1) near here, so I **don't see** (2) her very much. But we talk on the phone a lot. There's a youth centre in our neighbourhood. That's good! But it **doesn't open** (3) every day – only Mondays, Wednesdays, Fridays and Saturdays. Our neighbour, Mr Todd, isn't very friendly. I **don't know** (4) why. When I see him, he **doesn't say** (5) hello. Our other neighbour, Mrs Ortiz, also isn't very nice. She **doesn't like** (6) our dog, Millie. She says Millie is too noisy.

6 WORDS **Adjectives**

1 windy • 2 cloudy • 3 rainy • 4 snowy • 5 sunny

7 WRITING **Where I live**

Benutze die Checkliste um zu kontrollieren, ob du die Aufgabe erfüllt hast. Hast du etwas über die folgenden Themen geschrieben? Gib dir drei Punkte für jedes Thema, das du erwähnt hast.

			✓
Do you live in a village, city or town?	I live in a city/village/town. My city/village/town is …		
What is it like?	My town is … It's a … and … place. People are …	big • boring • clean • cold • cool • dirty • friendly • fun • interesting • loud • quiet • small • warm	
Some interesting or important places	In my neighbourhood there is/are … My town has … There is/are also … We don't have …	cafes • cinema • shops • hospital • houses • library • museum • park • restaurants • schools • skatepark • supermarket • swimming pool • trees • youth centre	
Some activities you can do	I like to … You can … My favourite activities are …	go shopping • go swimming • go to the library/museum • meet friends at a café / the park • play football/games • ride my bike • skateboard • watch films	
Things you (don't) like	I like my town because it's … I (don't) like … Sometimes it's too …	fun and interesting. the park/noise/big buildings. loud/quiet/cold.	

Total: _____ / 15

(*Lösungsbeispiel*)
Hi Conor,
Thanks for your mail. I want to answer your questions.
My town isn't very big, but it's a fun and interesting place. In my neighbourhood there are lots of nice houses and there are lots of trees too. It's very quiet but not boring. I like that. The town has a big park in the middle with a playground and a skatepark. That's really cool. I go there at the weekends with my friends. There's a cinema near the park too. We often go there. Sometimes we watch films in English! My favourite activities are swimming (there's a pool!) and skateboarding. I like my town because the people are friendly, it's clean, and it's not too big. What don't I like about it? We don't have a big shopping center with lots of shops.
Bye, Noel

8 MEDIATION
(*Lösungsbeispiel*)
1 Man ist drei Tage und zwei Nächte dort.
2 Man muss keine Erfahrung mitbringen. Die Surf-Lehrerinnen und Lehrer zeigen dir, wie es geht.
3 Nein, brauchst du nicht. Sie haben alles, was du brauchst.
4 Man bekommt Frühstück, Mittagessen und Abendessen.
5 Die Gruppen sind klein – zwischen 2 und 12 Leute.

9 SKILLS A short talk
1 talk about
2 this photo
3 let's look at
4 next
5 there
6 Thank
7 any questions

Wie kann ich mir Wörter besser merken?

Manche Wörter wollen einfach nicht im Gedächtmis bleiben! Dann können dir Merktechniken helfen:
- Schreibe das Wort auf einen Klebezettel und bringe ihn n einer Stelle an, wo du oft hinschaust.
- Male ein Bild zum Wort.
- Verbinde das Wort mit einer passenden Geste oder Bewegung.
- Suche passende Reimwörter: house – mouse
- Finde Wörter aus der gleichen Wortfamilie: dance – dancing, swim – swimmer
- Verwende das Wort in einem Satz oder einer typischen Redewendung: ride – ride a bike
- Finde Gegensatzpaare: sunny – rainy
- Finde Oberbegriff (umbrella words): football – sport, monkey – animal

Speaking

1 MONOLOGUE My favourites

(*Lösungsbeispiel*) Hello. My name is Wiebke. I'm 12 years old. I'm from Kiel. Now I live in Hamburg. My favourite animal is a monkey. They're interesting and very clever. My favourite hobby is taking photos. It's fun and some of my photos are great! My favourite place in my neighbourhood is the new swimming pool. It's cool and fun. I love swimming!

2 DIALOGUE At school (Unit 1)

(*Lösungsbeispiel*)

Partner A	Hi, Levi. How are you?
Partner B	I'm fine, thanks. What about you?
Partner A	I'm fine too. What's your next lesson?
Partner B	My next lesson is art. What about you?
Partner A	I have science. It's my favourite subject! What's your favourite subject?
Partner B	English. I have it on Tuesday for lessons three and four.
Partner A	Me too! So we're in the same class!
Partner B	Great! Are there any subjects you don't like?
Partner A	I don't like French. That's Thursday morning. What's your first lesson on Thursday?
Partner B	I have maths. It's not my favourite, but the teacher is nice.
Partner A	That's good. Well, it's time to go. I'll see you tomorrow in English class.
Partner B	See you!

> Alle Lösungsbeispiele aus diesem Kapitel kannst du aus deiner Cornelsen Lernen App abspielen.

3 DIALOGUE My dream home (Unit 2)

(*Lösungsbeispiel*)

Partner A	Is your dream home a house or a flat?
Partner B	It's a house. What about yours?
Partner A	My dream home is a flat. How big is your dream home?
Partner B	It's really big. It has 50 rooms!
Partner A	Wow! What rooms does it have?
Partner B	It has a big bedroom for me, of course, and rooms for all of my family and my friends. It has a sports hall and a garden with a swimming pool. The kitchen has a dining room table with enough chairs for everyone.
Partner A	Amazing! What about a living room?
Partner B	Yes, but the living room is a film room with 3 sofas and a big TV on the wall.
Partner A	I think I would like to come visit, please!
Partner B	I have a room for you! Now tell me about your dream home.
Partner A	It's a small flat in the city with just one room. The walls are all blue with white clouds. There's a kitchen with a small table and a big bed. The bed has lots of cushions on it. In the middle of the room, there's a drawing table where I can work.
Partner B	Does it have a garden?
Partner A	No, it's on the top floor.
Partner B	What's your favourite thing about your dream home?
Partner A	The drawing table is under a big window. I can look outside and see all the buildings in the city.

Lösungen

4 MONOLOGUE My friend (Unit 3)
🔊 12

(*Lösungsbeispiel*) I would like to talk about my penfriend, Shelly. Shelly is 12 years old and she lives in Brighton. She is funny and very nice. She has a cat and her cat's name is Pizza. She always eats the same thing for lunch: a sandwich and an apple. She never eats oranges. She likes coding and listening to music. She doesn't like the art or drawing. Her favourite sport is football and her favourite subject is computing.

5 MONOLOGUE Gracie's weekend (Unit 3, Unit 4)
🔊 13

(*Lösungsbeispiel*) I would like to tell you about Gracie's weekend. On Saturday morning, Gracie always sleeps late. She often eats Muesli or eggs for breakfast. Sometimes Gracie and her brother work in the garden with her dad. She likes working in the garden. Later, they often go to the supermarket. Gracie doesn't like shopping. In the afternoon, she always plays online video games with her friends. And she never goes to bed early on Saturdays.

On Sunday, Gracie gets up before the others. She often rides her bike to the park with her friends Abed and Lina. They play volleyball or football. Her family always has lunch together on Sunday. Sometimes they go visit Gracie's grandma in the afternoon. On Sunday evenings, Gracie and her brother always cook dinner. They have fun together. After dinner, Gracie and her family sometimes play board games. Gracie doesn't like board games.

6 DIALOGUE Let's meet! (Unit 3, Unit 4)
🔊 14

(*Lösungsbeispiel*)
Partner A Let's meet this weekend!
Partner B OK! What about the beach? We can go swimming.
Partner A Oh, I don't really like swimming. Let's go to the museum.
Partner B Hmm. OK. Do you want to get some ice cream too?
Partner A Yes, please! Are you free on Saturday afternoon?
Partner B I'm busy then. What about Sunday at 3 p.m.?
Partner A That's great. Let's meet at the ice cream shop next to the cinema.
Partner B Good idea! See you then!
Partner A Bye!

> *Let's talk* (Schulbuch, S. 205–212) enthält Wendungen für wichtige Situationen, wie z. B.: Über den Tagesablauf sprechen, sich verabreden.

7 MONOLOGUE A class picnic (Unit 5)
🔊 15

(*Lösungsbeispiel*) I see 2 teachers and a lot of students. They're having a picnic. A teacher, Mr. Harris, is cooking sausages. There's a table with a lot of food on it. I see some fruit and a chocolate cake. I see a cat under the table. I think the cat wants some food. The students are having fun at the picnic. Some of them are playing volleyball. Nick and Beth are sitting on the grass and playing cards. Ola is sitting in a tree. Leo is taking a photo of his friends.

Unit 5 Enjoy!

1 LISTENING Party time

Hörtext

Mum	Jada? Are you home?
Jada	Yes, I'm here, Mum. In the living room.
Mum	Ah, there you are. What are you doing?
Jada	I'm looking at my calendar.
Mum	Oh, that's perfect.
Jada	Why?
Mum	Because your birthday is in two weeks and I want to …
Jada	In two weeks? Are you sure? Saturday in two weeks is … the 6th of May. You're right, Mum! We need to plan my party!
Mum	What would you like to do for your party?
Jada	I'd like to have it in the garden, if the weather is nice, and play volleyball with my friends.
Mum	That's a good idea. What time would you like to start?
Jada	At 2 p.m.? Then we have lots of time.
Mum	OK. Let's make a shopping list for the food.
Jada	Food, yes! Can we make pizza?
Mum	Yes, of course. Then we need flour and tomato sauce and cheese and … What would you like on the pizza?
Jada	Well, you know I like salami.
Mum	Yes, I do. And what do your friends like?
Jada	I don't remember. But Selma is vegetarian. Can we make vegetarian pizza too?
Mum	Yes, sure. We can make it with vegetables. I'll put vegetables on the list.
Jada	Great! What about the cake?
Mum	I can make your favourite lemon cake.
Jada	I love lemon cake … but my friends like chocolate cake.
Mum	Or I can do something really different with strawberries.
Jada	That's a good idea! … Oh …. that's not a good idea.
Mum	Why not?
Jada	It's my friend Tim. He's allergic to strawberries.
Mum	Oh. Hm. Well, what about this? We can have a lemon cake and a chocolate cake. Then there's something for everybody.
Jada	That's it! You're the best, Mum!
Mum	Now, how many people would you like to invite?

Lösungen

🔊 07 **a)**
1. When Jada's mum comes home, Jada is …
   - ☐ a) playing a game.
   - ☑ b) looking at her calendar.
2. Jada would like to have her birthday party …
   - ☑ a) in the garden.
   - ☐ b) at the skatepark.
3. After they decide on the starting time, they …
   - ☐ a) start making pizzas.
   - ☑ b) make a shopping list.
4. They plan to have two cakes:
   - ☐ a) chocolate and strawberry.
   - ☑ b) lemon and chocolate.

🔊 07 **b)**
1. Jada's birthday is in two weeks, on **6th May**.
2. The party will start at **2 p.m.**
3. Jada's favourite kind of pizza is **salami**.
4. Jada's friend Selma is vegetarian, so Jada's mum will make some pizza with **vegetables**.
5. Tim is allergic to **strawberries**.

▶ Check

2 READING The garden party

	true	false
1 Jada and her friends aren't wearing shoes because it's summer.		✓
2 Selma is enjoying the vegetarian pizza.	✓	
3 Rajiv is drinking milk.		✓
4 Jada's dad isn't in the garden.	✓	
5 Ivan is thinking about food.	✓	
6 Mrs Gupta likes the music in the garden.		✓

3 WORDS Shopping list

strawberries — *d*
apples — *a*
eggs — *f*
tomatoes — *e*
butter — *b*
bread — *g*
sausages — *c*
cheese — *i*
salad — *h*
spaghetti — *j*

50 fifty

4 WORDS Our friends' birthdays

Birthdays	Beth says ...	Julio writes ...
2 Patrick: 12.3.	Patrick's birthday is in March.	12th March
3 Mina: 23.10.	Mina's birthday is in October.	23rd October
4 Khaled: 10.1.	Khaled's birthday is in January.	10th January
5 Luisa: 19.12.	Luisa's birthday is in December.	19th December
6 Henri: 26.5.	Henri's birthday is in May.	26th May
7 Soraya: 20.8.	Soraya's birthday is in August.	20th August

5 LANGUAGE That's not true!

2 No, she isn't **making** a cake. She's/she **is making** pizza.
3 No, it **isn't snowing**. It**'s raining**.
4 No, they **aren't playing** in the garden. They**'re sleeping** on the sofa / in the living room.
5 No, **you're not** writing an email. You**'re playing** videogames on your phone.
6 No, I**'m not watching** TV. I**'m finishing** this exercise.

> **!**
>
> Mit dem *present progressive* sagst du, was jemand jetzt gerade tut. Damit beschreibst du auch Bilder.
> Das *present progressive* besteht aus zwei Teilen:
>
> am/is/are + Verb + ing
>
> I**'m** learn**ing**
> you**'re** learn**ing**
> he/she/it**'s** learn**ing**
> we**'re** learn**ing**
> they**'re** learn**ing**

Lösungen

6 MEDIATION Baking with Dad
1. Wir brauchen Zucker, Butter, Eier, Mehl, Zitronen und Puderzucker.
2. Ja, das wird reichen.
3. Als erstes werden die Butter und der Zucker gemischt, dann kommen die Eier, das Mehl und der Saft einer Zitrone dazu.
4. Dann kommt die Mischung aus Puderzucker und dem restlichen Zitronensaft obendrauf.

7 WRITING A party invitation
Benutze die Checkliste um zu kontrollieren, ob du die Aufgabe erfüllt hast. Hast du etwas über die folgenden Themen geschrieben? Gib dir drei Punkte für jedes Thema, das du erwähnt hast.

		✓
Where the party is	My party is at …	
What day the party is	My party is on … It's on …	
What time the party starts and ends	from … to …	
Food and drinks	We can eat/drink … There's … to eat drink.	
3 Activities	We can play … There are lots activities like … The club has …	

Total: _____ / 15

(*Lösungsbeispiel*)
Hi Everybody!
It's my 12th birthday soon! My birthday party is at City Beach Club on 9th July from 2 p.m. to 6 p.m. We can eat pizza and drink lemonade and then there's chocolate cake for dessert! We have some fun activities too. There's party games, table tennis and, of course, swimming!
Please let me know if you can come or not. Hope to see you!
Anna

8 LANGUAGE Everything is fine

Sam We're/are doing great, Mum. How is the place where you are staying?
Mum It's OK. At the moment I'm/am having some tea in the hotel dining room. What about you?
Sam I'm/am helping with dinner. The chicken is cooking in the oven. I'm so hungry.
Mum That's nice. What else is for dinner?
Sam Joel is making rice and peas.
Mum What? Your brother is cooking? That's new. Where's your dad?
Sam Dad's outside. He's/is working in the garden.
Mum I see. What about the dogs?
Sam They're/are playing in the garden. Everything is great, Mum.

Unit 4
Where I live

1 LISTENING It's their first time here ____/11 ▶ SB, p. 105

a) Navid is Alma's neighbour. Navid's cousins are visiting and he wants to do some fun things with them. He asks Alma for some tips. Listen and number the places in the right order.
Navid ist Almas Nachbar. Navids Cousin und Cousine sind zu Besuch und Navid will einiges mit ihnen unternehmen. Er fragt Alma nach Tipps. Höre zu und nummeriere die Orte in der richtigen Reihenfolge. (5 Punkte)

- Lies dir immer die Aufgabe vor dem Anhören durch. Du kannst dann gezielter zuhören.
- Oft geben die Überschrift oder die Bilder schon erste Hinweise auf den Inhalt eines Listening-Textes.

b) Listen again. Complete the sentences with the missing word or words.
Höre noch einmal zu. Vervollständige die Sätze mit dem fehlenden Wort oder mit den fehlenden Wörtern. (6 Punkte)

1. Navid hopes that the weather on Saturday is warm and _____.
2. Alma sometimes goes to the _____.
3. Navid's cousin Mina doesn't _____ very much.
4. Alma knows a fish and chips shop _____ the pier.
5. They can sit _____ if the weather isn't _____.

▶ Check

4

2 WORDS In town ____ / 8
▶ SB, pp. 105–109

Match the words with the right description. Draw lines.
Verbinde die Wörter mit der richtigen Definition. Ziehe Linien.

1 dirty
2 cinema
3 swap
4 ice rink
5 marina
6 neighbourhood
7 stadium
8 village

A There are lots of boats there.
B It's a place to go skating.
C It's too small to be a city or a town.
D It's a place where you can watch a football game.
E When something isn't clean.
F When you give something to somebody and take something different.
G It's a place where you can watch a film.
H The place where you and your neighbours live.

3 LANGUAGE New in town ____ / 15
▶ SB, p. 111, p. 114, pp. 180–181

Erklär-film

a) **Nadia is new in town. She has some questions for her classmate, Josie. Complete Nadia's questions with *Do* or *Does*. Then complete Josie's answers with *do, does, don't* or *doesn't*.**
Nadia ist neu in der Stadt. Sie hat einige Fragen an ihre Klassenkameradin, Josie. Vervollständige Nadias Fragen mit Do *oder* Does *und Josie's Antworten mit* do, does, don't *oder* doesn't. *(10 Punkte)*

1 _____ you know a good clothes shop? – Yes, I _____.

2 _____ the sports centre open on Sundays? – Yes, it _____.

3 _____ the buses stop at the school? – Yes, they _____.

4 _____ the town have a stadium? – No, it _____.

5 _____ you have a favourite chips shop? – No, I _____.

Erklär-film

b) **Nadia has more questions. Use the words from the box to complete her questions. You don't need one of the words.** *Nadia hat mehr Fragen. Benutze die Fragewörter aus dem Kasten, um ihre Fragen zu vervollständigen. Eins der Wörter brauchst du nicht. (5 Punkte)*

When • Where • Why • Who • How • What

1 _____ do the shops close? – At 8 o'clock.

2 _____ do kids go on Saturday afternoons to play? – The park.

3 _____ often do you go to the cinema? – Every weekend!

4 _____ time do you walk to the bus in the morning? – At 7:45.

5 _____ do you go to school by bus when your house is so near? – Because I love buses!

! **who and where**
Bei **who** and **where** musst du immer gut aufpassen.
Who heißt auf deutsch „wer" und **where** heißt auf Deutsch „wo".

▶ Check

4 Reading Where am I?   ____ / 8   ▶ SB, p. 116, p. 192

These friends like playing a guessing game when they're at different places. Read their messages.
Diese Freunde spielen gerne ein Ratespiel, wenn sie an unterschiedlichen Orten sind. Lies ihre Texte.

Iris
OK, guys. People often come to this place in the evening, but I like to go on Sunday afternoon. You buy a ticket inside or online and you can buy snacks too. Then in a big room a film starts and you sit and watch. Where am I? ✓

Aisha
This is a very cool place. It's outside and it doesn't cost money. I can bring my skateboard here and have a lot of fun. Today there aren't many people here. That's good because it's hard to skateboard when it's really full. Where am I? ✓

Max
I am here because I need to buy some clothes and other things. There are lots of different shops here in one big building. I like that. Some people here don't shop – they meet their friends or watch the other shoppers. Where am I? ✓

a) Guess where each person is. Choose from the places in the box and complete the sentences.
Rate, wo jede Person ist. Benutze die Orte im Kasten und vervollständige die Sätze. (3 Punkte)

1 Iris is at the _____.
2 Aisha is _____.
3 Max is _____.

> beach • cinema • museum • shopping centre • skatepark • stadium • supermarket

b) Read the text messages again. True or false? Tick (✓).
Lies die Texte noch einmal. Richtig oder falsch? Markiere (✓). (5 Punkte)

	true	false
1 Where Iris is, people like to go in the evening.		
2 Aisha is at a fun place that costs money.		
3 It's really full, where Aisha is.		
4 Max is there to shop for clothes.		
5 Where Max is, not everybody wants to shop.		

▶ Check

4

5 LANGUAGE Neighbours ____ / 12   ▸ SB, p. 111, p. 180

a) Many people in the neighbourhood like talking about the weather. Complete their sentences with *don't* or *doesn't*.
Viele Leute in der Nachbarschaft reden gerne über das Wetter. Vervollständige ihre Sätze mit don't *oder* doesn't. *(7 Punkte)*

1. I often cycle to school, but I _____ take my bike when it's windy. It's too hard to ride!
2. Sandy and Leo _____ need sunny weather to go windsurfing. When it's cloudy and grey outside, that _____ stop them.
3. Brighton _____ often get hot in May, but today it's 26 degrees. I _____ like it!
4. The Brighton Pier _____ close when it's cold and snowy. It stays open in all weather.
5. Most people _____ go out when it's rainy, but I like walking on the beach.

b) Complete Ada's negative statements about her neighbourhood with *don't* or *doesn't* and the verbs in brackets.
Vervollständige Adas verneinte Aussagen über ihre Nachbarschaft mit don't *oder* doesn't *und den Verben in Klammern. (5 Punkte)*

My friend Zofia *doesn't live* (1 live) near here, so I _____ (2 see) her very much. That's a shame. There's a youth centre in our neighbourhood. That's good! But it _____ (3 open) every day – only Mondays, Wednesdays, Fridays and Saturdays. Our neighbour Mr Todd isn't very friendly. I _____ (4 know) why. When I see him, he _____ (5 say) hello. Our other neighbour, Mrs Ortiz, also isn't very nice. She _____ (6 like) our dog, Millie. She says Millie is too noisy.

6 WORDS Adjectives ____ / 5   ▸ SB, p. 114, pp. 225–229

What's the word to describe the weather?
Welches Wort beschreibt das Wetter?

1. w_____
2. c_____
3. r_____
4. s_____
5. s_____

7 WRITING Where I live   ____ / 15   ▶ More help, p. 76 ▶ SB, p. 106, p. 192

You get an email from your Irish penfriend, Conor. He tells you all about his town. Read the last part of his email.
Du bekommst eine E-Mail von deinem irischen Brieffreund Conor. Er erzählt dir alles über seine Stadt. Lies den letzten Teil seiner E-Mail.

> And that's my town! It's small and it has some problems, but there are some great places and cool things to do here too.
> What about your town? Or is it a village? I want to know more about it!
> What does your neighbourhood look like?
> What are some activities that you can do there?
> What do you like and what don't you like about it?
> Sorry, that's a lot of questions. :-)
>
> Write back soon!
>
> Bye, Conor

Write an email to Conor and answer his questions. You can use the ideas in the boxes.
Schreibe eine E-Mail an Conor und beantworte seine Fragen. Du kannst die Ideen in den Kästen benutzen.

museum • library • cinema • youth centre • clothes shop • building • park • supermarket • hospital • skatepark • …	clean • dirty • loud • quiet • warm • cold • cool • interesting • fun • go shopping • watch films • go to the park • …

Hi Conor,

Thanks for your mail. I want to answer your questions.

My town is/isn't _____

In my neighbourhood there is/there are _____
_____

It's _____
_____

The town has _____
_____

There's _____
_____

My favourite activities you can do here are _____
_____

Bye, _____

▶ Check

8 MEDIATION Surfing in Cornwall ____ / 5 ▶ SB, p. 113

Your family wants to go to Cornwall for a holiday. You go online and find this interesting website. You describe it to your parents in German. Answer their questions.

Deine Familie will einen Urlaub in Cornwall machen. Du gehst online und findest diese interessante Webseite. Du beschreibst sie auf Deutsch für deine Eltern. Beantworte ihre Fragen.

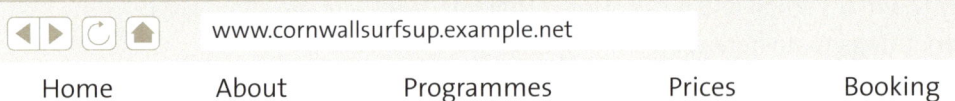www.cornwallsurfsup.example.net

Home   About   Programmes   Prices   Booking

Cornwall Surfing Holiday

Have a wild weekend by the sea with three days of surfing! If you don't know know how to surf, you can learn with our great surf teachers. It's a great summer weekend of fun!

Where: Newquay, Cornwall

Highlights
- You get three surf lessons.
- We have all the things you need for your surf lesson.
- Our teachers are the best.
- The groups are small: 2–12 people.
- There's lots of time to practise surfing.
- You stay three days near the beach.
- We give you breakfast, lunch and dinner.

Check-in time: 4:30 p.m. on Friday
Check-out time: 1:00 p.m. on Sunday
You can find out more about when it is and how much it costs <u>here</u>.

1 Wie viele Tage und Nächte ist man dort?
   _____ .

2 Kann man mitmachen, wenn man noch nie surfen war?
   _____ .

3 Müssen wir zum Surfen etwas mitbringen?
   _____ .

4 Was ist mit dem Essen? Wie wird das organisiert?
   _____ .

5 Wie groß sind die Gruppen?
   _____ .

▶ Check

9 SKILLS A short talk ____ / 7   ▶ SB, p. 120, p. 171–172

Look at Aisha's short talk and complete her statements with the correct words and phrases from the box.
Schaue Aishas Vortrag an und vervollständige ihre Aussagen mit den richtigen Wörtern und Satzteile aus dem Kasten.

> any questions • let's look at • next • talk about • Thank • there • this photo

Today I'd like to _____ (1) my neighbourhood. I live in Stanford Avenue in Brighton. It's a really cool part of Brighton. In _____ (2) you can see some houses. Our house is the one with the two big trees. Now _____ (3) these pictures of the neighbourhood. Here is Blakeley Park. It's near our house. It's a great park for basketball and for tennis. I go there a lot with my friends. The _____ (4) photo shows the library. I can walk there in three minutes. You can see that it's a big building. And the last photo shows the food shop where we do our shopping. I always meet friendly neighbours _____ (5). And that's my neighbourhood! _____ (6) you. Do you have _____ (7)?

Bereich	Aufgabe	erreichte Punktzahl	🤩	😎	🤔	😭
listening	1	____ / 11	11–10	9–8	7–6	5–0
reading	4	____ / 8	8–7	6	5–4	3–0
words	2 6	____ / 8 ____ / 5 } ____ / 13	13–12	11–9	8–7	6–0
language	3 5	____ / 15 ____ / 12 } ____ / 27	27–24	23–19	18–14	13–0
writing	7	____ / 15	15–14	13–11	10–8	7–0
mediation	8	____ / 5	5	4	3	2–0
skills	9	____ / 7	7	6–5	4	3–0
Gesamt		____ / 86	86–78	77–61	60–43	42–0

▶ Check

Speaking

1 MONOLOGUE My favourites ▶ SB, pp. 14–16, p. 196

a) Plan a short talk about yourself and your favourite things. First write the answers to the questions below. *Bereite einen kurzen Vortrag über dich selbst vor. Schreibe als erstes die Antworten zu diesen Fragen auf.*

Nimm dich beim Üben auf. Danach kannst du kontrollieren, ob du wirklich alles gesagt hast, was du sagen wolltest.

What's your name? _____   How old are you? _____

Where are you from? _____   Where do you live? _____

b) Make a list of your favourite things. Write your favourites on the left side of the table. On the right side, write some words that describe your favourites. You can use the words in the box. *Stelle eine Liste deiner Lieblingssachen zusammen. Schreibe deine Lieblingssachen auf die linke Seite der Tabelle. Notiere auf der rechten Seite Wörter, um sie zu beschreiben. Du kannst die Wörter im Kasten benutzen.*

> active • big • blue • clever • cool • cute • different • fast • friendly • free • fun • funny • great • hard • interesting • modern • new • nice • old • perfect • quiet • small • special • sweet

My favourite ...	It's ...
animal	
hobby	
thing	
subject	
place in my neighbourhood	
food	

c) Give a short talk about yourself. Introduce yourself with the information in part a). Then talk about three of your favourite things using your notes from part b). *Halte einen kurzen Vortrag über dich selbst. Stelle dich mit den Informationen aus a) vor. Sprich dann über drei deiner Lieblingssachen aus b).*

> Hello. My name is Wiebke. I'm 12 years old. I'm from Kiel. Now I live in Hamburg. My favourite animal is a monkey. They're interesting and very clever. My favourite hobby is ...

Speaking

2 DIALOGUE At school (Unit 1)

▶ SB, pp. 26–27, pp. 197–198

It's Monday, the first day of the school year, and you and your partner meet during morning break. Say hello and ask how your partner is. Then ask questions about your partner's timetable. Partner A asks questions first. Use the timetables below to answer your partner's questions.

Es ist Montag, der erste Tag des neuen Schuljahres, und du triffst in der Pause eine Freundin oder einen Freund. Sage hallo und frage wie es ihr/ihm geht. Stelle dann Fragen zum Stundeplan. Partner A fragt zuerst. Benutze die Stundenpläne unten um die Fragen zu beantworten.

Ask about:
- the next lesson
- favourite subjects
- subjects he/she doesn't like
- when your partner has art/English/…
- the first/last lesson on Monday/Tuesday/…

Wenn du Dialoge üben willst, finde ein Gegenüber, mit dem du zusammen üben kannst, am besten aus deinem Englischkurs. Du kannst auch eine Person um Hilfe bitten, die Englisch spricht, zum Beispiel Freunde oder Familie.

Partner A's timetable

Lesson	Monday	Tuesday	Wednesday	Thursday	Friday
1	art	maths	art	French	science
2	geography	history	PE	French	history
Break					
3	science	English	music	science	computing
4	computing	English	geography	science	computing
Lunch					
5	PE	German	maths	English	English
6	PE	design and technology	maths	design and technology	PE

A: Hi, (name). How are you?
B: I'm fine, thanks. What about you?
A: I'm fine too. What's your next lesson?
B: My next lesson is science/art… What about you?
A: I have …

Partner B's timetable

Lesson	Monday	Tuesday	Wednesday	Thursday	Friday
1	geography	German	PE	maths	English
2	computing	maths	music	maths	science
Break					
3	art	English	art	science	French
4	music	English	geography	science	French
Lunch					
5	design and technology	PE	computing	art	design and technology
6	history	PE	computing	history	PE

▶ Check

Speaking

🔊 11 **3 DIALOGUE My dream home (Unit 2)** ▶ SB, pp. 50–51, p. 190, pp. 196–197

a) Take a moment to think about your dream home. Make notes about the topics below.
Nimm dir etwas Zeit und denke über dein Traumzuhause nach. Mache Notizen zu den untenstehenden Themen.

- if it's a house or a flat
- how big it is
- the different rooms
- things in the rooms and where they are
- other places like a garden
- favourite places and things

b) With a partner take turns asking and answering questions about dream homes. You can use the ideas in the box. *Stelle deiner Partnerin oder deinem Partner abwechselnd Fragen zu eurem Traumzuhause. Ihr könnt die Ideen im Kasten benutzen.*

> Is it …? • Is/Are there …? • What about …? • What's your favourite …? • It has … • There is/are …
> bathroom • bedroom living room • dining room • games room • garden • hall • kitchen • office
> • toilet • bed • chair • computer • cushions • desk • lamp • poster • shelves • sofa • table • TV •
> wardrobe • behind • in • in front of • next to • on • under

You can start like this:
A: Is your dream home a house or a flat?
B: It's a … What about yours?
A: My dream home is a … How big is your dream home?
B: It's really big. It has … rooms.

🔊 12 **4 MONOLOGUE My friend (Unit 3)** ▶ SB, pp. 79–80, p. 179

This is your English penfriend. Look at the photo and the information. Write some more information about her. Then talk about her. You should answer the following questions:
Das ist deine englische Brieffreundin. Schaue das Foto und die Infos an. Schreibe noch mehr Infos über sie. Dann sprich über sie. Du solltest folgende Fragen beantworten:

- How old is she? _____
- Where does she live? _____
- What is she like? _____
- Does she have a pet? _____
- What does she eat? _____
- What's her favourite hobby/sport/subject? _____
- What's does/doesn't she like? (colours/foods/animals/…)

Name: Shelly
Age: 12
From: Brighton, England

The ideas from the boxes can help you.

> Her name is … • She's … years old. •
> She lives in … • She is … • She has … •
> She often eats … • Her favourite … is … •
> She likes … • She doesn't like…

> art • apples • sandwiches • cat • coding • funny •
> hamsters • her bike • listening to music • maths •
> nice • pizza • purple

▶ Check

Speaking

5 MONOLOGUE Gracie's weekend (Unit 3, Unit 4) ▶ SB, pp. 80–84, p. 179, pp. 198–199

Gracie does different activities at the weekend. There are some activities that she likes and some that she doesn't like. Look at the pictures and the information and talk about Gracie's weekend.
Gracie macht verschiedene Sachen am Wochenende. Manche Aktivitäten mag sie und manche nicht. Schaue die Bilder und Informationen an und rede über Gracies Wochenende.

You can start like this:
On Saturday morning, Gracie usually sleeps late. She often …

Saturday

morning • always • late • sleep   often • muesli • breakfast • eat   sometimes • Gracie and her brother • dad • garden • help

later • often • go to supermarket • brother 😟   afternoon • always • play online video games • friends   evening • never • go to bed • early[1]

Sunday

morning • before the others • get up   often • cycle • Abed and Lina • park • volleyball or football   always • have lunch • together • family

afternoon • sometimes • visit • grandma 🙂   evening • cook • Gracie and her brother • dinner • always   sometimes • board games • family • play 😟

▶ Check

[1] **early** *früh*

Speaking

6 DIALOGUE Let's meet! (Unit 3, Unit 4) ▶ SB, pp. 86–87, pp. 198–199

a) You and your partner want to meet at the weekend. Before you start, you look at the pictures. Each of you writes down two places that you would like to go. *Zu zweit möchtet ihr euch am Wochenende verabreden. Bevor ihr anfangt, schaut die Bilder an. Jede/r schreibt zwei Orte auf, wo sie/er hingehen möchte.*

b) Talk to your partner. Ask and answer questions about:
 – Where do you want to go?
 – What day and time do you want to meet?

Sprecht miteinander und entscheidet:
 – *Wohin möchtet ihr gehen?*
 – *An welchem Tag und zu welcher Uhrzeit wollt ihr euch treffen?*

You can use the ideas in the boxes or your own.

> **!**
> **at** the cinema
> **at** 2 p.m.
> **on** Saturday
> **on** Sunday

Ask to meet	Say *yes*	Say *no*
Let's go to the park / the shopping centre.	I'd love to.	I have a different idea.
Let's meet at the museum / the beach.	Good idea!	That's not my favourite place.
We can see/buy/eat/play/get …	Yes, please!	No, thanks.
What about a film / some ice cream?	Yes, I like …	Oh, I don't really like …
Do you want to …?	OK.	Sorry I can't.
Are you free on Saturday / at 2 p.m.?	That's great.	I'm busy then.

You can start like this:
Partner A: Let's meet this weekend!
Partner B: OK! Do you want to …?
Partner B: Hmm. I have a different idea. What about …?
Partner A: Good idea! It's really nice there. We can …

▶ Check

Speaking

7 MONOLOGUE A class picnic (Unit 5)

▶ SB, pp. 138–139, pp. 141–142

It's a warm Friday in June and class 7E are having their class picnic in the park. Look at the picture and talk about it. Describe the people in the picture. *Es ist ein warmer Freitagnachmittag im Juni und Klasse 7E macht ihr Sommerpicknick im Park. Schaue dir das Bild an und rede darüber.*

Make sure to answer the following questions:

- What can you see?
- Who can you see?
- Where are they in the picture?
- What are they doing?
- What food can you see on the table?

> cook • drink • eat • play • read • sit • read • ...

> ball • cake • cat • dog • drinks • fruit • game • sausages • tree • volleyball • ...

I see 2 teachers and a lot of students. They're having a picnic. A teacher, Mr. Harris, is cooking sausages. There's a table with a lot of food on it. I see ...

Höre dir die Lösungsbeispiele an und achte nicht nur auf den Inhalt, sondern auch auf Aussprache und Intonation.

▶ Check

Unit 5
Enjoy!

1 LISTENING Party time _____ / 9 ▶ SB, pp. 136–137

a) **Read the task carefully. Then listen to the conversation between Jada and her mum and tick (✓) the right answer.** *Lies die Aufgabe sorgfältig durch. Höre dann das Gespräch zwischen Jada und ihrer Mutter an und markiere (✓) die richtige Antwort. (4 Punkte)*

1 When Jada's mum comes home, Jada is …
- [ ] a) playing a game.
- [ ] b) looking at her calendar.

2 Jada would like to have her birthday party …
- [ ] a) in the garden.
- [ ] b) at the skatepark.

3 After they decide on the starting time, they …
- [ ] a) start making pizzas.
- [ ] b) make a shopping list.

4 They plan to have two cakes:
- [ ] a) chocolate and strawberry.
- [ ] b) lemon and chocolate.

b) **Read the task, then listen again to the dialogue and answer the questions.**
Lies die Aufgabe. Höre dir den Dialog an und beantworte die Fragen. (5 Punkte)

1 Jada's birthday is in two weeks, on _____.

2 The party will start at _____.

3 Jada's favourite kind of pizza is _____.

4 Jada's friend Selma is vegetarian so Jada's mum will make some pizza with _____.

5 Tim is allergic to _____.

▶ Check

2 READING The garden party ____ / 6

▶ SB, pp. 138–139, pp. 146–148

Read about Jada's birthday party and answer: true or false? Tick (✓)
Lies über Jadas Geburtstagsfeier und antworte: richtig oder falsch? Markiere (✓) (6 Punkte)

It's 3:30 on a Saturday afternoon and a lot is happening[1] in Jada's garden. It's May, but it's so warm that it feels like summer. That's why Jada and most of her friends aren't wearing any shoes.

Music is playing and there's a big picnic table with lots of food and drinks on it. Jada's friend Selma is eating her vegetarian pizza and she's complimenting Jada's mum.

"This pizza is so good!", Selma tells her.

Tim is on the other side of the table. He's eating some pizza and talking to Rajiv. Rajiv is drinking some lemonade. Tim is allergic to strawberries and Rajiv is allergic to milk.

unbekannte Wörter aus dem Text erschließen
Dieser Text enthält einige unbekannte Wörter, die du dir aber aus dem Zusammenhang erschließen kannst.

They're happy because there is a lot at the party that they can eat and drink. Rajiv is looking at the chocolate cake. "I think I'm ready for some dessert," Rajiv says.

Jada and her friends Mara, Felix and Ivan are playing volleyball. Mara and Ivan are winning the game. Ivan is getting hungry.

"The next point wins the game! OK?", he says.

Jada's dad is in front of the house. He's talking to their neighbour, Mrs Gupta. Mrs Gupta isn't happy about the music in the garden.

"Please, Mrs. Gupta, the kids are having fun, and the party ends at 5 o'clock. Please come in and have some lemon cake and tea," he says.

"Well ... maybe just one piece of cake," she says.

		true	false
1	Jada and her friends aren't wearing shoes because it's summer.		
2	Selma is enjoying the vegetarian pizza.		
3	Rajiv is drinking milk.		
4	Jada's dad isn't in the garden.		
5	Ivan is thinking about food.		
6	Mrs Gupta likes the music in the garden.		

▶ Check

---

[1] **happen** *geschehen, passieren*

5

3 Words Shopping list ___ / 9
▶ SB, p. 141–142, p. 193

After food shopping, Denis and his dad are checking their shopping list. Match the food and drinks on the table with the ones on the list.
Nach dem Einkauf prüfen Denis und sein Vater ihre Einkaufsliste. Ordne die Lebensmittel auf dem Tisch denen auf der Liste zu.

strawberries	d
apples	___
eggs	___
tomatoes	___
butter	___
bread	___
sausages	___
cheese	___
salad	___
spaghetti	___

4 Words Our friends' birthdays ___ / 12
▶ SB, pp. 136–137, p. 258

Beth and Julio are trying to remember their friends' birthdays. Beth is reading the months to Julio, and he is writing the dates down.
Beth und Julio versuchen, sich die Geburtstage ihrer Freunde zu merken. Beth liest die Monate und Julio schreibt die Tage auf.

Birthdays	Beth says …	Julio writes …
1 Ariel: 5.7.	Ariel's birthday is in *July* .	*5th July*
2 Patrick: 12.3.	Patricks birthday is in _____ .	_____
3 Mina: 23.10.	Mina's birthday is in _____ .	_____
4 Khaled: 10.1.	Khaled's birthday is in _____ .	_____
5 Luisa: 19.12.	Luisa's birhtday is in _____ .	_____
6 Henri: 26.5.	Henri's birthday is in _____ .	_____
7 Soraya: 20.8.	Soraya's Birthday is in _____ .	_____

▶ Check

5 LANGUAGE That's not true! ___ / 10

▶ SB, p. 138, p. 182

Look at the pictures and correct the mistakes in the mini dialogues. Complete the sentences with the present progressive. *Schaue die Bilder an und korrigiere die Aussagen. Vervollständige die Sätze in den Mini-Dialogen mit dem present progressive (2 Punkte pro Antwort)*

1 Zak and Ruth are eating burgers.

No, they *aren't eating* burgers. They're *eating* spaghetti.

2 Manuela is making a cake.

No, she _____ a cake. She _____ pizza.

3 It is snowing.

No, it _____ snowing. It _____ raining.

4 Sam's dogs are playing in the garden.

No, they _____ in the garden.

They _____ on the sofa.

5 I'm writing an email.

No, you _____ an email.

You _____ video games on your phone.

6 You're watching TV. (finish / this exercise)

No, I _____ TV. I _____ .

6 Mediation Baking with Dad ___ / 8   ▶ SB, p. 144, p. 154

For your birthday party you want to bake a lemon cake together with your dad. You find a recipe on a UK cooking website. Answer your dad's questions about the recipe in German.

Für deine Geburtstagsfeier willst du zusammen mit deinem Vater einen Zitronenkuchen backen. Du findest ein Rezept auf einer englischen Webseite. Beantworte seine Fragen zum Rezept auf Deutsch.

www.melissaskitchen.example.net

Melissa's Kitchen   Home   Recipes   Baking   Health   Vegetarian

Yummy Lemon Cake

Hey guys! Lemon Cake is one of my favourite desserts. It's so yummy and it's great for parties. Lemon Cake is really simple to make too. With this recipe you can make your own yummy Lemon Cake.

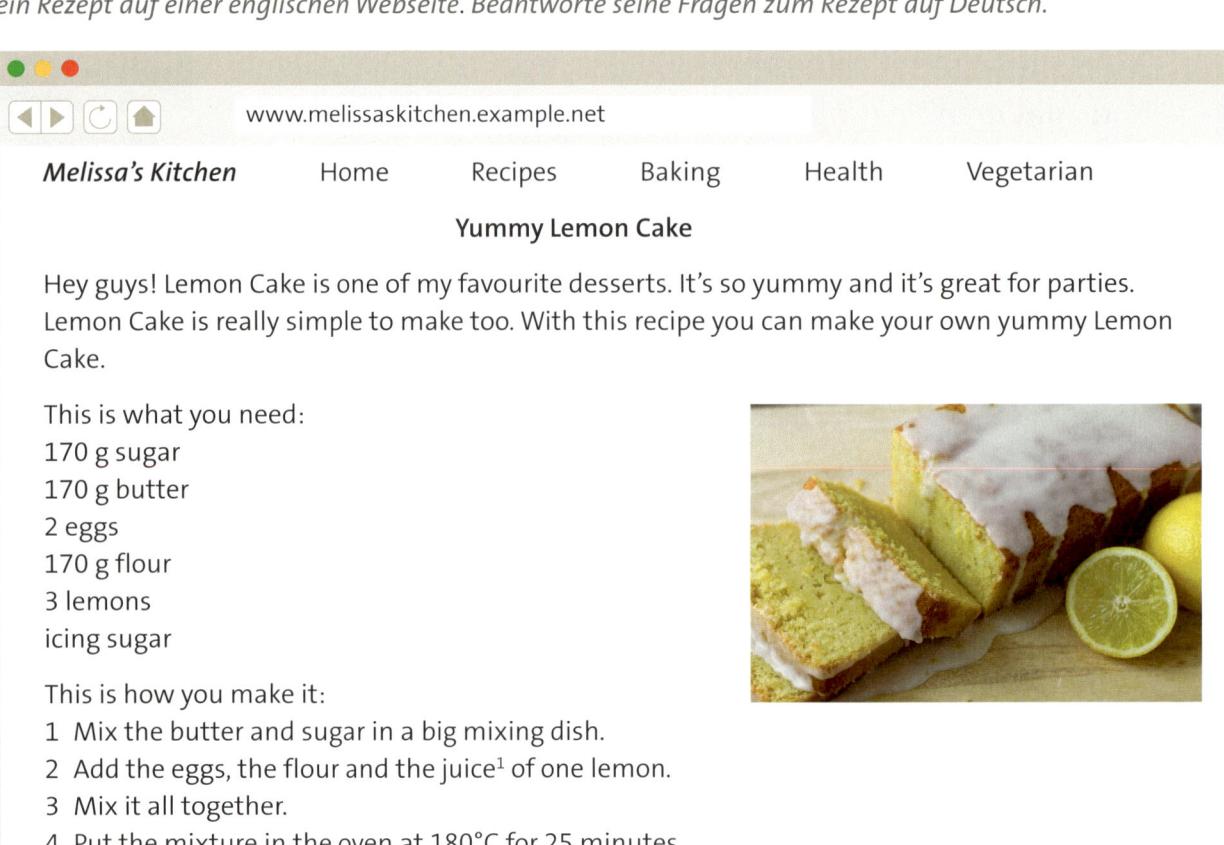

This is what you need:
170 g sugar
170 g butter
2 eggs
170 g flour
3 lemons
icing sugar

This is how you make it:
1 Mix the butter and sugar in a big mixing dish.
2 Add the eggs, the flour and the juice[1] of one lemon.
3 Mix it all together.
4 Put the mixture in the oven at 180°C for 25 minutes.
5 When the cake is cool, put the icing sugar and the juice of two lemons in a pan and stir.
6 When it's hot, pour[2] the mixture over the cake.
7 Let it cool. Done!

Papa: OK, welche Zutaten brauchen wir?
Du: _____. (1)

Papa: Super! Wir haben alles da, aber wir haben nur drei Eier und drei Zitronen. Wird das reichen?
Du: _____. (2)

Papa: Mischen wir zuerst die Eier und das Mehl oder wie?
Du: _____. (3)

Papa: Nachdem wir den Kuchen aus dem Ofen geholt haben, was kommt noch obendrauf?
Du: _____. (4)

▶ Check

[1] **juice** *Saft*   [2] **pour** *gießen*

7 WRITING A party invitation ____ / 15

▶ More Help, p. 77   ▶ SB, p. 136

Anna has a lot to do for her birthday party. Help her write her party invitation. Include the information in the pictures for
- when
- where
- food and drinks
- activities.

Anna hat viel zu tun für ihre Geburtstagsfeier. Hilf ihr, die Einladung zu schreiben. Beachte die Informationen auf den Bildern zu
- *wann*
- *wo*
- *Essen und Getränke*
- *Aktivitäten.*

Hi Everybody!

It's my 12th birthday soon! My party is _____

_____

We can eat _____

_____

We have some fun activities too. There's _____

_____

Please let me know if you can come or not. Hope to see you!

Anna

▶ Check

5

8 LANGUAGE Everything is great ____ / 8   ▶ SB, p. 138, p. 182

Sam's mum is travelling for work. She is talking to Sam on the phone. Complete their statements with the correct form of the present progressive.

Sams Mutter ist auf Geschäftsreise. Sie telefoniert mit Sam. Vervollständige ihre Aussagen mit der korrekten Form des present progressive.

Sam: We _____ (do) great, Mum. How is the place where you _____ (stay)?

Mum: Yes, I am. At the moment I _____ (have) a cup of tea in the hotel dining room. What about you?

Sam: Nothing, really. I _____ (help) with dinner. The chicken _____ (cook) in the oven. I'm so hungry.

Mum: That's nice. What else is for dinner?

Sam: Joel _____ (make) rice and peas.

Mum: Joel is cooking? That's new. Where's your dad?

Sam: Dad's outside. He _____ (work) in the garden.

Mum: I see. What about the dogs?

Sam: They _____ (play) in the garden. Everything is great, Mum.

Bereich	Aufgabe	erreichte Punktzahl	🤩	😎	🤔	😭
listening	1	___ / 9	9–8	7–6	5	4–0
reading	2	___ / 6	6	5	4–3	2–0
words	3 4	___ / 9 ___ / 12 } ___ / 19	19–17	16–13	12–10	9–0
language	5 8	___ / 10 ___ / 8 } ___ / 18	18–17	16–13	12–9	8–0
mediation	6	___ / 8	8–7	6	5–4	3–0
writing	7	___ / 15	15–14	13–11	10–8	7–0
Gesamt		___ / 75	75–68	67–53	52–38	37–0

▶ Check

More help

▶ Unit 1, page 15

9 WRITING An email to a friend   ____ / 15   ▶ SB, p. 26–27

Write an email to your English friend Jamie. Tell him about your school.
Schreibe deinem englischen Freund Jamie eine E-Mail. Erzähle ihm von deiner Schule.

You can write about:
- your timetable
- your favourite subjects
- what you like at school
- your teachers
- your friends at school
- ...

You can use the phrases in the box. *Du kannst die Ideen im Kasten benutzen.*

> The name of my school is ... • I'm in class ... • My timetable is very good/easy/difficult/full. •
> I have English/history/science on Monday/Tuesday/ ... • On Monday my first/last lesson is ... •
> My favourite subject is ... • I also like ... • It's fun/interesting.
> I (don't) like kids/teachers/canteen at my school. • The art room / sports hall is great. •
> My (favourite) teacher is ... • She's/He's my art/maths teacher • She's/He's nice/helpful/OK.
> My best friend is in the same / in a different / in my music class. • My school friends are brave/clever/cool.

---

to   Jamie@example.net
subject My school

Hi Jamie,

Today I want to write to you about my school. The name of my school is _____.

I'm in class _____. My favourite teacher is _____.

He/She _____. The kids at my school are/aren't _____.

My timetable is very _____. My favourite lesson is _____.

My friends at school are _____.

Thats my school!

Bye,

▶ Check

seventy-three 73

More help

▶ Unit 2, page 21

10 WRITING Email to a friend   ___ / 15   ▶ SB, p. 51, pp. 215–217

Arun gets an email from his penfriend Mara. She tells him about her flat. She wants to know more about his home. Write Arun's email and describe his house.

Arun bekommt eine E-Mail von seiner Brieffreundin Mara. Sie erzählt ihm von ihrer Wohnung. Sie will mehr über sein Zuhause wissen. Schreibe Aruns E-Mail und beschreibe sein Haus.

Answer the following questions:
- What are the rooms like? (big, small, nice, etc.)
- Where is the kitchen? (next to / …)
- Where is your room?

The words and phrases in the box can help you:

| big • cool • different • messy • modern • nice • small • tidy |
| behind • in • in front of • next to • under |
| bathroom • dining room • garden • hall • kitchen • living room • my bedroom • office • parents' bedroom |

My room is …
There's a … garden.
The bathroom is next to the…

Hi Mara,

Thanks for your email! I can tell you about my house. I live in _____

_____

My house is _____

There is _____

And there are _____

_____

I really like _____

What do you think? _____

Write back soon!
Arun

▶ Check

74 seventy-four

▶ Unit 3, page 26

7 Writing **My Saturday** ____ / 15   ▶ SB, pp. 79–80

Write about a normal Saturday for you and your family at home. You can use words or phrases from the two boxes. Write six sentences or more.

Schreibe über einen normalen Samstag bei dir zu Hause. Du kannst die Wörter und Satzteile aus den Kästen benutzen. Schreibe sechs oder mehr Sätze.

Schreibe, **wann** jemand etwas tut. Du kannst auch sagen, **wie häufig, mit wem** und/oder **warum** jemand etwas tut. Sammele vorher deine Ideen wie folgt:

wann	wer	wie häufig	was	wo / mit wem / warum
After breakfast	I	always	play football	in the park.
	My mum		go shopping	with my dad.
In the afternoon	My brother and I	sometimes	draw pictures	because it's fun.

at … o'clock • at the weekend • before/after … • in the morning/afternoon/evening • on Saturday • then	get up • have a shower • get dressed • eat/have/make … for breakfast/lunch/dinner • tidy up • meet with … • play games/sport/music • go cycling/swimming/shopping/… • do art/coding/yoga… • watch TV / a film • read a book/magazine/newspaper • text with friends • go to bed at …

A normal Saturday for me begins at about _____ a.m. That's when I get up. After that, I _____

_____

Then I like to _____

Sometimes I _____

After _____

_____

We have lunch at _____ Sometimes I eat _____

_____

In the afternoon, _____

_____

After dinner _____

I go to bed at _____

More help

▶ Unit 4, page 57

7 Writing Where I live ____ / 15 ▶ SB, p 106, p. 192

You get an email from your Irish penfriend, Conor. He tells you all about his town. Read the last part of his email.
Du bekommst eine E-Mail von deinem irischen Brieffreund Conor. Er erzählt dir alles über seine Stadt. Lies den letzten Teil seiner E-Mail.

> And that's my town! It's small and it has some problems, but there are some great places and cool things to do here too.
> What about your town? Or is it a village? I want to know more about it!
> What does your neighbourhood look like? What are some activities that you can do there?
> What do you like and what don't you like about it?
> Sorry, that's a lot of questions. :-) Write back soon!
>
> Bye, Conor

Write an email to Conor and answer his questions. You can use the ideas in the boxes.
Schreibe eine E-Mail an Conor und beantworte seine Fragen. Du kannst die Ideen in den Kästen benutzen.

| museum • library • cinema • youth centre • clothes shop • building • park • supermarket • hospital • skatepark • ... | clean • dirty • loud • quiet • warm • cold • cool • interesting • fun • go shopping • watch films • go to the park • ... |

> Hi Conor,
>
> Thanks for your mail. I want to answer your questions.
>
> My town isn't very _____, but it's _____.
>
> In my neighbourhood there are _____.
>
> The town has _____. That's really cool.
>
> There is/are also _____.
>
> My favourite activities that you can do are _____.
>
> I also like to _____.
>
> I like my town because _____.
>
> But I don't like _____.
>
> Bye, _____

▶ Check

More help

▶ Unit 5, page 71

7 WRITING A party invitation   ___ / 15   ▶ SB, p. 136

Anna has a lot to do for her birthday party. Help her write her party invitation. Include the information in the pictures for
- when
- where
- food and drinks
- activities.

Anna hat viel zu tun für ihre Geburtstagsfeier. Hilf ihr, die Einladung zu schreiben. Beachte die Informationen auf den Bildern zu
- *wann*
- *wo*
- *Essen und Getränke*
- *Aktivitäten.*

City Beach Club

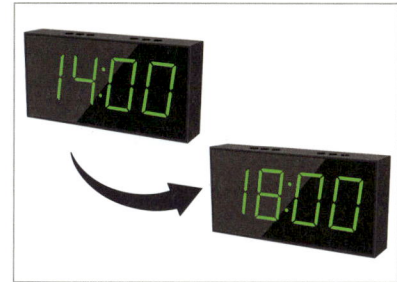

at (a place) • on (a day) • from (a start time) to (an end time) • We can eat/drink/play … • There's … to eat/drink. • There are lots of activities like … • The club has …	cake • lemonade • party games • swimming • table tennis • 2 p.m. • 6 p.m. • 9th July

Hi Everybody!

It's my 12th birthday soon! My party is at _____ on _____

from _____ to _____

_____

We can eat _____ and then there's _____

_____

We have some fun activities. There's _____

_____

Please let me know if you can come or not. Hope to see you!

Anna

▶ Check

So bereitest du dich auf eine Arbeit vor

Damit du dich optimal auf eine Klassenarbeit vorbereiten kannst, musst du lernen, wie du richtig lernst. Das richtige Lernen bzw. Üben wird nicht von der Zahl der bearbeiteten Aufgaben, sondern viel mehr von der Lernatmosphäre und der Strukturierung des Lernprozesses, beeinflusst.

Die Lernatmosphäre vorbereiten

Eine ruhige, druckfreie Lernatmosphäre ist wichtig. Beim Lernen handelt es sich um eine bewertungsfreie Situation, in der das Üben im Vordergrund stehen soll. Es sollte dir möglich sein, angst- bzw. sorgenfrei **Fehler** zu machen und **Fragen** zu stellen. Dies ist wichtig für deinen Lernfortschritt. **Pausen** gehören zum Lernprozess, denn sie helfen eine kognitive Überforderung zu verhindern. Auf eine 45-minütige Übungseinheit kann z.B. eine fünf- bis zehnminütige (Bewegungs-)Pause folgen.

Lerninhalte für die Klassenarbeit

Für eine erfolgreiche Vorbereitung ist es wichtig, die **Lerninhalte der Klassenarbeit** zu kennen. Du solltest dich daher mindestens eine Woche vor der Klassenarbeit bei der Fachlehrkraft informieren. Wenn du schon früher mit der Vorbereitung beginnen willst, kannst du im Inhaltsverzeichnis des Schülerbuchs (S. 4-9) nachschauen. Es besitzt eine ausführliche Übersicht über die Kompetenzen und sprachlichen Mittel (*vocabulary* & *grammar*), die du in jeder Unit vermittelt bekommst.

Ergänzende Materialien

Neben dem Klassenarbeitstrainer solltest du ein separates **Lernheft** führen. Dort kannst du die Arbeitsergebnisse zu den Aufgaben festhalten und so jede Aufgabe mehrfach bearbeiten.

Manchmal ist es ebenfalls hilfreich **eine Lernpartnerin oder einen Lernpartner** in der Klasse zu suchen. Ihr könnt euch unterstützen und bei Fragen und Problemen gegenseitig helfen.

Um keine der relevanten Kompetenzen zu vergessen, solltest du einen **Lernplan** erstellen. In diesem kannst du festhalten, was, wann geübt werden soll. Du kannst auch zusätzliche Übungsmöglichkeiten oder hilfreiche Schulbuchseiten notieren. Das Abhaken geübter Kompetenzen gibt dir einen Überblick über den Lernprozess bis zur Klassenarbeit. So könnte ein ausgefüllter Lernplan für Unit 2 aussehen:

Kompetenz / I can…	Sprachliche Mittel	Materialien	Wann übe ich das?	Erledigt?	Noch mal üben?
… talk about my family	Voc family words, … is my brother/ stepmum.	SB, p. 44-45 Wordbank p. 189	Mo. 20.11.	✓	nein
… talk about pets	Voc pets, My favourite pet is … because …	Pets: SB, pp. 46-49 Wordbank, p. 190 Vocabulary, p. 214	Mo. 20.11.	✓	ja, am Do. 23.11.
… talk about pets	G to be (questions and short answers)	to be: SB, p. 47 Language file, p. 178 Erklärfilm in der Cornelsen Lernen App	Di. 21.11.	✓	nein

Lernplan

> Um dich gut auf die kommende Englischarbeit vorzubereiten, solltest du dich frühzeitig informieren, welche Themen in der Arbeit drankommen. Damit du nichts vergisst und auch genug Zeit hast, um zu lernen, solltest du dir einen Lernplan erstellen. Du kannst diesen Plan als Vorlage nutzen:

Lernplan von: _____

Datum der Klassenarbeit: _____

Unit 1 / 2 / 3 / 4 / 5

Kompetenz / I can...	Sprachliche Mittel	Materialien	Wann übe ich das? (Datum)	Erledigt? (✓)	Noch mal üben? (ja/nein)

Quellenverzeichnis

Titelbild
Cornelsen/Personen: Anja Poehlmann, Brighton Pier: mauritius images/Steve Vidler

Illustrationen
Cornelsen/Evelt Yanait, Advocate Art: S. 9–12; S. 16; S. 17 u.r.; S. 19+20; S. 23 3.1–3.3; S. 24; S. 26; S. 38; S. 50; S. 56; S. 59 o.r.+m.r.; S. 63; S. 65 m.; S. 67+68; S. 72 m.r.; S. 74; **Cornelsen/Irina Zinner:** S. 5 o.; S. 27+29 (Lösungen); S. 73; S. 75

Abbildungen
S. 1 Siehe S. 10, S. 30, S. 60; **S. 5** 1–5: Cornelsen/Anja Poehlmann; **S. 6** 1: Shutterstock.com/dore art, 2: Shutterstock.com/Raksha Shelare, 3: stock.adobe.com/TODOS LOS DERECHOS RESERVADOS/Luis, 4: stock.adobe.com/Prostock-studio, headphones: Shutterstock.com/Noch, TV: Shutterstock.com/zcreamz11, person: Shutterstock.com/ksenvitaln, book: Shutterstock.com/zcreamz11, pool: Shutterstock.com/Noch; **S. 7** 1: Shutterstock.com/juan carlos tinjaca, 2: Shutterstock.com/Lubo Ivanko, 3: stock.adobe.com/Kirill Gorlov, 4: stock.adobe.com/StockPhotoPro, 5: stock.adobe.com/VaLiza/valiza14; **S. 7** m.l.: Shutterstock.com/Pla2na, m.r.: stock.adobe.com/bahadirbermekphoto, u.l.: Imago Stock&People GmbH/Westend61, u.r.: mauritius images/SuperStock; **S. 8** 1: stock.adobe.com/Sainam, 2: stock.adobe.com/PUTSADA, 3: stock.adobe.com/Lunja, 4: stock.adobe.com/chamnan phanthong, 5: Shutterstock.com/veronika serkopova, 6: stock.adobe.com/NaturePhoto/ondrejprosicky; **S. 11** u.r.: Shutterstock.com/Monkey Business Images; **S. 13** 1: Imago Stock&People GmbH/Loop Images/Highwaystarz, 2: Shutterstock.com/Monkey Business Images, 3: stock.adobe.com/Roman, 4: Shutterstock.com/Monkey Business Images; **S. 14** 1: stock.adobe.com/peopleimages.com/Nina Lawrenson, 2: stock.adobe.com/Robert Kneschke, 3: mauritius images/alamy stock photo/Valerii Honcharuk, 4: Shutterstock.com/Monkey Business Images, 5: stock.adobe.com/lev dolgachov/Syda Productions, school things: Shutterstock.com/kai Keisuke, people oben: Shutterstock.com/Monkey Business Images, people unten: stock.adobe.com/Tom Wang, subjects links (Calculator and circle tool): mauritius images/alamy stock photo/Lasse Kristensen, subjects rechts (globe): Shutterstock.com/SrideeStudio, places oben: Shutterstock.com/Monkey Business Images, places unten: stock.adobe.com/Dean Hindmarch/dglimages; **S. 15** emoticons: Shutterstock.com/Yefym Turkin; **S. 17** o.r.: stock.adobe.com/Cultura Creative; **S. 18** bird + lizard: Shutterstock.com/Eric Isselee, snake: Shutterstock.com/bluedog studio, horse: stock.adobe.com/dul_ny, hamsters: stock.adobe.com/fotomaster, rabbit: stock.adobe.com/voren1, fishes: stock.adobe.com/anusorn, dog: Shutterstock.com/MaraZe; **S. 21** emoticons: Shutterstock.com/Yefym Turkin; **S. 22** A: mauritius images/alamy stock photo/Champa Bangari, B: stock.adobe.com/LIGHTFIELD STUDIOS, C: stock.adobe.com/milatas, D: stock.adobe.com/pololia; **S. 23** 1: Shutterstock.com/Rendra Dria Septia Aji, 2+3: Shutterstock.com/Azizah's, 4: Shutterstock.com/HPL17; **S. 25** 1: Imago Stock&People GmbH/Westend61, 2: Shutterstock.com/Arvind Balaraman, 3: stock.adobe.com/Alena Ozerova, 4: Depositphotos/Dmitrii Marchenko, 5: stock.adobe.com/IndiaPix, 6: Shutterstock.com/4 PM production, emoticons: Shutterstock.com/Yefym Turkin; **S. 27** emoticons: Shutterstock.com/Yefym Turkin; **S. 30** 2: Shutterstock.com/Raksha Shelare, 3: stock.adobe.com/TODOS LOS DERECHOS RESERVADOS/Luis, 4: stock.adobe.com/Prostock-studio, book: Shutterstock.com/zcreamz11, headphones: Shutterstock.com/Noch, TV: Shutterstock.com/zcreamz11, person: Shutterstock.com/ksenvitaln, pool: Shutterstock.com/Noch; **S. 41**: Shutterstock.com/Yefym Turkin; **S. 53** A: stock.adobe.com/THINK b, B: stock.adobe.com/Mark, C: stock.adobe.com/Diana Vyshniakova, D: stock.adobe.com/Bene Images, E: stock.adobe.com/arenaphotouk; **S. 54**: Shutterstock.com/Olena Yakobchuk; **S. 55** m.r.: Shutterstock.com/Dina Morozova; **S. 55** o.l.: stock.adobe.com/anastasy_helter; **S. 55** o.r.: stock.adobe.com/Lazy_Bear; **S. 58**: Shutterstock.com/Image Source Collection; **S. 59** emoticons: Shutterstock.com/Yefym Turkin; **S. 60**: stock.adobe.com/byswat; **S. 61**: Shutterstock.com/SpeedKingz; **S. 62**: Shutterstock.com/Ground Picture; **S. 63** emoticons: Shutterstock.com/Yefym Turkin; **S. 64** 6.1: stock.adobe.com/Lucky Business, 6.2: stock.adobe.com/Roman Milert, 6.3: Shutterstock.com/kornnphoto, 6.4: stock.adobe.com/snvv, 6.5: stock.adobe.com/Kirk Fisher, 6.6: stock.adobe.com/Lyudmila; **S. 65** u.l.: stock.adobe.com/Shot-Pixel/Olga Yastremska/Leonid Yastremskiy; **S. 66**: Shutterstock.com/Bonezboyz; **S. 69** 1: stock.adobe.com/ulianna19970, 2: stock.adobe.com/Photographee.eu, 3: stock.adobe.com/pingpao, 4: mauritius images/EyeEm, 5: stock.adobe.com/Drobot Dean; **S. 70**: stock.adobe.com/Kirsty Begg/gourmetphotography; **S. 71+77** o.l.: Depositphotos/Olesya Shelomova, o.m.: stock.adobe.com/Alena, o.r.: stock.adobe.com/Azizah, Pfeil: stock.adobe.com/fotohansel, Kuchen: Shutterstock.com/October22, Sandwich: Shutterstock.com/Asya Nurullina, Limo: Shutterstock.com/JeniFoto, m.: stock.adobe.com/IdeaBug, Inc./Rosemarie Gearhart, m.r.: Shutterstock.com/New Africa,; **S. 72** emoticons: Shutterstock.com/Yefym Turkin